THIS BOOK BELONGS TO:

CONTACT INFORMATION	
NAME:	
ADDRESS:	
PHONE:	

START / END DATES

/ / TO / /

DEDICATION

This book is dedicated to all the ones that love Pizza!

You are my inspiration in producing books and I'm excited to help in the planning of your next pizza order.

How to Use this Pizza Review Log Book:

The purpose of this Pizza Review Notebook is to keep all your various pizza eating adventures organized in one easy to find spot.

Here are some simple guidelines to follow so you can make the most of using this book:

1. The first "Pizza" section is for you to write out the date, the pizzeria, neighborhood, beverage pairing and all information in one spot and more..so you can go back there to be reminded of your journey.

2. Most ideas are inspired by something we have seen. Use the "Toppings" section to write down all the information about your topping choices, whether it's cheese, pineapple, green pepper and so much more.

3. The "Cheese" section is for you to write out whether it's greasy, stringy, creamy, salty with checkboxes and much more.

4. And even more pages with the "Sauce" section is great for writing out the taste you prefer whether it's tangy, sweet, savory, stinky, salty with checkboxes so you can be reminded later.

5. The "Freshness" section is for you to rate from 1 to 5 how fresh the pizza tasted to you and all things you think about your pizzas along the way.

6. And finally, use this "Crust" section to check off if you like the buttery crust, spongy crust, chewy and what size crust you prefer as well.

Enjoy!

Pizza Log

DATE	
PIZZERIA	
NEIGHBORHOOD	

TOPPINGS

○ CHEESE	○ MUSHROOMS	○ ONIONS
○ PINEAPPLE	○ BACON	○ TUNA
○ GREEN PEPPER	○ SAUSAGE	○ BLACK OLIVES
○ OTHER		

CHEESE

○ GREASY	○ STINGY
○ SMOKEY	○ STINKY
○ CREAMY	○ SALTY

SAUCE

○ SWEET	○ SAVORY
○ TANGY	○ SPICY
○ THIN	○ CHUNKY

CHEESE TO SAUCE RATIO (CSR)

CHEESE	☐☐☐☐☐☐☐
SAUCE	☐☐☐☐☐☐☐

FRESHNESS

○1 ○2 ○3 ○4 ○5

CRUST SIZE

○ THIN
○ MEDIUM
○ LARGE

CRUST

○ BUTTERY	○ CRISPY
○ SPONGY	○ BUBBLY
○ CHEWY	○ OTHER

CRUST

○1 ○2 ○3 ○4 ○5

STYLE ○ NY ○ CHICAGO ○ OTHER

COMMENTS

MY RATING ○1 ○2 ○3 ○4 ○5 ○6 ○7 ○8 ○9 ○10

EAT AGAIN? ○ YES ○ NO

Pizza Log

DATE	
PIZZERIA	
NEIGHBORHOOD	

TOPPINGS		
○ CHEESE	○ MUSHROOMS	○ ONIONS
○ PINEAPPLE	○ BACON	○ TUNA
○ GREEN PEPPER	○ SAUSAGE	○ BLACK OLIVES
○ OTHER		

CHEESE	
○ GREASY	○ STINGY
○ SMOKEY	○ STINKY
○ CREAMY	○ SALTY

SAUCE	
○ SWEET	○ SAVORY
○ TANGY	○ SPICY
○ THIN	○ CHUNKY

CHEESE TO SAUCE RATIO (CSR)	
CHEESE	☐☐☐☐☐☐☐
SAUCE	☐☐☐☐☐☐☐

FRESHNESS

○ 1 ○ 2 ○ 3 ○ 4 ○ 5

CRUST SIZE	CRUST	
○ THIN	○ BUTTERY	○ CRISPY
○ MEDIUM	○ SPONGY	○ BUBBLY
○ LARGE	○ CHEWY	○ OTHER

CRUST

○ 1 ○ 2 ○ 3 ○ 4 ○ 5

STYLE	○ NY ○ CHICAGO ○ OTHER

COMMENTS

MY RATING	○1 ○2 ○3 ○4 ○5 ○6 ○7 ○8 ○9 ○10	EAT AGAIN?	○ YES ○ NO

Pizza Log

DATE	
PIZZERIA	
NEIGHBORHOOD	

TOPPINGS

○ CHEESE	○ MUSHROOMS	○ ONIONS
○ PINEAPPLE	○ BACON	○ TUNA
○ GREEN PEPPER	○ SAUSAGE	○ BLACK OLIVES
○ OTHER		

CHEESE

○ GREASY	○ STINGY
○ SMOKEY	○ STINKY
○ CREAMY	○ SALTY

SAUCE

○ SWEET	○ SAVORY
○ TANGY	○ SPICY
○ THIN	○ CHUNKY

CHEESE TO SAUCE RATIO (CSR)

CHEESE	☐ ☐ ☐ ☐ ☐ ☐ ☐
SAUCE	☐ ☐ ☐ ☐ ☐ ☐ ☐

FRESHNESS

○1 ○2 ○3 ○4 ○5

CRUST SIZE

○ THIN
○ MEDIUM
○ LARGE

CRUST

○ BUTTERY	○ CRISPY
○ SPONGY	○ BUBBLY
○ CHEWY	○ OTHER

CRUST

○1 ○2 ○3 ○4 ○5

STYLE ○ NY ○ CHICAGO ○ OTHER

COMMENTS

MY RATING ○1 ○2 ○3 ○4 ○5 ○6 ○7 ○8 ○9 ○10

EAT AGAIN? ○ YES ○ NO

Pizza Log

DATE	
PIZZERIA	
NEIGHBORHOOD	

TOPPINGS

○ CHEESE	○ MUSHROOMS	○ ONIONS
○ PINEAPPLE	○ BACON	○ TUNA
○ GREEN PEPPER	○ SAUSAGE	○ BLACK OLIVES
○ OTHER		

CHEESE

○ GREASY	○ STINGY
○ SMOKEY	○ STINKY
○ CREAMY	○ SALTY

SAUCE

○ SWEET	○ SAVORY
○ TANGY	○ SPICY
○ THIN	○ CHUNKY

CHEESE TO SAUCE RATIO (CSR)

CHEESE	☐☐☐☐☐☐☐
SAUCE	☐☐☐☐☐☐☐

FRESHNESS

○1 ○2 ○3 ○4 ○5

CRUST SIZE	CRUST	
○ THIN	○ BUTTERY	○ CRISPY
○ MEDIUM	○ SPONGY	○ BUBBLY
○ LARGE	○ CHEWY	○ OTHER

CRUST

○1 ○2 ○3 ○4 ○5

STYLE	○ NY ○ CHICAGO ○ OTHER

COMMENTS

MY RATING	○1 ○2 ○3 ○4 ○5 ○6 ○7 ○8 ○9 ○10	EAT AGAIN?	○ YES ○ NO

Pizza Log

DATE	
PIZZERIA	
NEIGHBORHOOD	

TOPPINGS

O CHEESE	O MUSHROOMS	O ONIONS
O PINEAPPLE	O BACON	O TUNA
O GREEN PEPPER	O SAUSAGE	O BLACK OLIVES
O OTHER		

CHEESE

O GREASY	O STINGY
O SMOKEY	O STINKY
O CREAMY	O SALTY

SAUCE

O SWEET	O SAVORY
O TANGY	O SPICY
O THIN	O CHUNKY

FRESHNESS

O1 O2 O3 O4 O5

CHEESE TO SAUCE RATIO (CSR)

CHEESE	☐☐☐☐☐☐☐
SAUCE	☐☐☐☐☐☐☐

CRUST SIZE

O THIN
O MEDIUM
O LARGE

CRUST

O BUTTERY	O CRISPY
O SPONGY	O BUBBLY
O CHEWY	O OTHER

CRUST

O1 O2 O3 O4 O5

STYLE O NY O CHICAGO O OTHER

COMMENTS

MY RATING	O1 O2 O3 O4 O5 O6 O7 O8 O9 O10	EAT AGAIN? O YES O NO

Pizza Log

DATE	
PIZZERIA	
NEIGHBORHOOD	

TOPPINGS

○ CHEESE	○ MUSHROOMS	○ ONIONS
○ PINEAPPLE	○ BACON	○ TUNA
○ GREEN PEPPER	○ SAUSAGE	○ BLACK OLIVES
○ OTHER		

CHEESE

○ GREASY	○ STINGY
○ SMOKEY	○ STINKY
○ CREAMY	○ SALTY

SAUCE

○ SWEET	○ SAVORY
○ TANGY	○ SPICY
○ THIN	○ CHUNKY

CHEESE TO SAUCE RATIO (CSR)

CHEESE	□ □ □ □ □ □ □
SAUCE	□ □ □ □ □ □ □

FRESHNESS

○ 1 ○ 2 ○ 3 ○ 4 ○ 5

CRUST SIZE

○ THIN
○ MEDIUM
○ LARGE

CRUST

○ BUTTERY	○ CRISPY
○ SPONGY	○ BUBBLY
○ CHEWY	○ OTHER

CRUST

○ 1 ○ 2 ○ 3 ○ 4 ○ 5

STYLE ○ NY ○ CHICAGO ○ OTHER

COMMENTS

MY RATING	○1 ○2 ○3 ○4 ○5 ○6 ○7 ○8 ○9 ○10	**EAT AGAIN?**	○ YES ○ NO

Pizza Log

DATE	
PIZZERIA	
NEIGHBORHOOD	

TOPPINGS

○ CHEESE	○ MUSHROOMS	○ ONIONS
○ PINEAPPLE	○ BACON	○ TUNA
○ GREEN PEPPER	○ SAUSAGE	○ BLACK OLIVES
○ OTHER		

CHEESE

○ GREASY	○ STINGY
○ SMOKEY	○ STINKY
○ CREAMY	○ SALTY

SAUCE

○ SWEET	○ SAVORY
○ TANGY	○ SPICY
○ THIN	○ CHUNKY

CHEESE TO SAUCE RATIO (CSR)

CHEESE	☐☐☐☐☐☐☐
SAUCE	☐☐☐☐☐☐☐

FRESHNESS

○1 ○2 ○3 ○4 ○5

CRUST SIZE

○ THIN
○ MEDIUM
○ LARGE

CRUST

○ BUTTERY	○ CRISPY
○ SPONGY	○ BUBBLY
○ CHEWY	○ OTHER

CRUST

○1 ○2 ○3 ○4 ○5

STYLE ○ NY ○ CHICAGO ○ OTHER

COMMENTS

MY RATING ○1 ○2 ○3 ○4 ○5 ○6 ○7 ○8 ○9 ○10

EAT AGAIN? ○ YES ○ NO

Pizza Log

DATE	
PIZZERIA	
NEIGHBORHOOD	

TOPPINGS		
○ CHEESE	○ MUSHROOMS	○ ONIONS
○ PINEAPPLE	○ BACON	○ TUNA
○ GREEN PEPPER	○ SAUSAGE	○ BLACK OLIVES
○ OTHER		

CHEESE	
○ GREASY	○ STINGY
○ SMOKEY	○ STINKY
○ CREAMY	○ SALTY

SAUCE	
○ SWEET	○ SAVORY
○ TANGY	○ SPICY
○ THIN	○ CHUNKY

CHEESE TO SAUCE RATIO (CSR)	
CHEESE	☐☐☐☐☐☐☐
SAUCE	☐☐☐☐☐☐☐

FRESHNESS

○ 1 ○ 2 ○ 3 ○ 4 ○ 5

CRUST SIZE	CRUST	
○ THIN	○ BUTTERY	○ CRISPY
○ MEDIUM	○ SPONGY	○ BUBBLY
○ LARGE	○ CHEWY	○ OTHER

CRUST

○ 1 ○ 2 ○ 3 ○ 4 ○ 5

STYLE	○ NY ○ CHICAGO ○ OTHER

COMMENTS

MY RATING	○1 ○2 ○3 ○4 ○5 ○6 ○7 ○8 ○9 ○10	EAT AGAIN?	○ YES ○ NO

Pizza Log

DATE	
PIZZERIA	
NEIGHBORHOOD	

TOPPINGS

O CHEESE	O MUSHROOMS	O ONIONS
O PINEAPPLE	O BACON	O TUNA
O GREEN PEPPER	O SAUSAGE	O BLACK OLIVES
O OTHER		

CHEESE

O GREASY	O STINGY
O SMOKEY	O STINKY
O CREAMY	O SALTY

SAUCE

O SWEET	O SAVORY
O TANGY	O SPICY
O THIN	O CHUNKY

CHEESE TO SAUCE RATIO (CSR)

CHEESE	☐☐☐☐☐☐☐
SAUCE	☐☐☐☐☐☐☐

FRESHNESS

O1 O2 O3 O4 O5

CRUST SIZE

O THIN
O MEDIUM
O LARGE

CRUST

O BUTTERY	O CRISPY
O SPONGY	O BUBBLY
O CHEWY	O OTHER

CRUST

O1 O2 O3 O4 O5

STYLE	O NY O CHICAGO O OTHER

COMMENTS

MY RATING	O1 O2 O3 O4 O5 O6 O7 O8 O9 O10	EAT AGAIN?	O YES O NO

Pizza Log

DATE	
PIZZERIA	
NEIGHBORHOOD	

TOPPINGS		
○ CHEESE	○ MUSHROOMS	○ ONIONS
○ PINEAPPLE	○ BACON	○ TUNA
○ GREEN PEPPER	○ SAUSAGE	○ BLACK OLIVES
○ OTHER		

CHEESE	
○ GREASY	○ STINGY
○ SMOKEY	○ STINKY
○ CREAMY	○ SALTY

SAUCE	
○ SWEET	○ SAVORY
○ TANGY	○ SPICY
○ THIN	○ CHUNKY

CHEESE TO SAUCE RATIO (CSR)	
CHEESE	☐☐☐☐☐☐☐
SAUCE	☐☐☐☐☐☐☐

FRESHNESS

○ 1 ○ 2 ○ 3 ○ 4 ○ 5

CRUST SIZE	CRUST	
○ THIN	○ BUTTERY	○ CRISPY
○ MEDIUM	○ SPONGY	○ BUBBLY
○ LARGE	○ CHEWY	○ OTHER

CRUST

○ 1 ○ 2 ○ 3 ○ 4 ○ 5

STYLE	○ NY ○ CHICAGO ○ OTHER

COMMENTS

MY RATING	○1 ○2 ○3 ○4 ○5 ○6 ○7 ○8 ○9 ○10	EAT AGAIN?	○ YES ○ NO

Pizza Log

DATE	
PIZZERIA	
NEIGHBORHOOD	

TOPPINGS

○ CHEESE	○ MUSHROOMS	○ ONIONS
○ PINEAPPLE	○ BACON	○ TUNA
○ GREEN PEPPER	○ SAUSAGE	○ BLACK OLIVES
○ OTHER		

CHEESE

○ GREASY	○ STINGY
○ SMOKEY	○ STINKY
○ CREAMY	○ SALTY

SAUCE

○ SWEET	○ SAVORY
○ TANGY	○ SPICY
○ THIN	○ CHUNKY

CHEESE TO SAUCE RATIO (CSR)

CHEESE	□□□□□□□
SAUCE	□□□□□□□

FRESHNESS

○1 ○2 ○3 ○4 ○5

CRUST SIZE

○ THIN
○ MEDIUM
○ LARGE

CRUST

○ BUTTERY	○ CRISPY
○ SPONGY	○ BUBBLY
○ CHEWY	○ OTHER

CRUST

○1 ○2 ○3 ○4 ○5

STYLE ○ NY ○ CHICAGO ○ OTHER

COMMENTS

MY RATING ○1 ○2 ○3 ○4 ○5 ○6 ○7 ○8 ○9 ○10

EAT AGAIN? ○ YES ○ NO

Pizza Log

DATE	
PIZZERIA	
NEIGHBORHOOD	

TOPPINGS		
○ CHEESE	○ MUSHROOMS	○ ONIONS
○ PINEAPPLE	○ BACON	○ TUNA
○ GREEN PEPPER	○ SAUSAGE	○ BLACK OLIVES
○ OTHER		

CHEESE	
○ GREASY	○ STINGY
○ SMOKEY	○ STINKY
○ CREAMY	○ SALTY

SAUCE	
○ SWEET	○ SAVORY
○ TANGY	○ SPICY
○ THIN	○ CHUNKY

CHEESE TO SAUCE RATIO (CSR)	
CHEESE	☐ ☐ ☐ ☐ ☐ ☐ ☐
SAUCE	☐ ☐ ☐ ☐ ☐ ☐ ☐

FRESHNESS

○ 1 ○ 2 ○ 3 ○ 4 ○ 5

CRUST SIZE	CRUST	
○ THIN	○ BUTTERY	○ CRISPY
○ MEDIUM	○ SPONGY	○ BUBBLY
○ LARGE	○ CHEWY	○ OTHER

CRUST

○ 1 ○ 2 ○ 3 ○ 4 ○ 5

STYLE	○ NY ○ CHICAGO ○ OTHER

COMMENTS

MY RATING	○1 ○2 ○3 ○4 ○5 ○6 ○7 ○8 ○9 ○10	EAT AGAIN?	○ YES ○ NO

Pizza Log

DATE	
PIZZERIA	
NEIGHBORHOOD	

TOPPINGS

○ CHEESE	○ MUSHROOMS	○ ONIONS
○ PINEAPPLE	○ BACON	○ TUNA
○ GREEN PEPPER	○ SAUSAGE	○ BLACK OLIVES
○ OTHER		

CHEESE

○ GREASY	○ STINGY
○ SMOKEY	○ STINKY
○ CREAMY	○ SALTY

SAUCE

○ SWEET	○ SAVORY
○ TANGY	○ SPICY
○ THIN	○ CHUNKY

CHEESE TO SAUCE RATIO (CSR)

CHEESE	☐ ☐ ☐ ☐ ☐ ☐ ☐
SAUCE	☐ ☐ ☐ ☐ ☐ ☐ ☐

FRESHNESS

○ 1 ○ 2 ○ 3 ○ 4 ○ 5

CRUST SIZE

○ THIN
○ MEDIUM
○ LARGE

CRUST

○ BUTTERY	○ CRISPY
○ SPONGY	○ BUBBLY
○ CHEWY	○ OTHER

CRUST

○ 1 ○ 2 ○ 3 ○ 4 ○ 5

STYLE ○ NY ○ CHICAGO ○ OTHER

COMMENTS

MY RATING ○ 1 ○ 2 ○ 3 ○ 4 ○ 5 ○ 6 ○ 7 ○ 8 ○ 9 ○ 10

EAT AGAIN? ○ YES ○ NO

Pizza Log

DATE	
PIZZERIA	
NEIGHBORHOOD	

TOPPINGS

○ CHEESE	○ MUSHROOMS	○ ONIONS
○ PINEAPPLE	○ BACON	○ TUNA
○ GREEN PEPPER	○ SAUSAGE	○ BLACK OLIVES
○ OTHER		

CHEESE

○ GREASY	○ STINGY
○ SMOKEY	○ STINKY
○ CREAMY	○ SALTY

SAUCE

○ SWEET	○ SAVORY
○ TANGY	○ SPICY
○ THIN	○ CHUNKY

CHEESE TO SAUCE RATIO (CSR)

CHEESE	☐☐☐☐☐☐☐
SAUCE	☐☐☐☐☐☐☐

FRESHNESS

○1 ○2 ○3 ○4 ○5

CRUST SIZE

○ THIN
○ MEDIUM
○ LARGE

CRUST

○ BUTTERY	○ CRISPY
○ SPONGY	○ BUBBLY
○ CHEWY	○ OTHER

CRUST

○1 ○2 ○3 ○4 ○5

STYLE ○ NY ○ CHICAGO ○ OTHER

COMMENTS

MY RATING ○1 ○2 ○3 ○4 ○5 ○6 ○7 ○8 ○9 ○10

EAT AGAIN? ○ YES ○ NO

Pizza Log

DATE	
PIZZERIA	
NEIGHBORHOOD	

TOPPINGS

○ CHEESE	○ MUSHROOMS	○ ONIONS
○ PINEAPPLE	○ BACON	○ TUNA
○ GREEN PEPPER	○ SAUSAGE	○ BLACK OLIVES

○ OTHER

CHEESE

○ GREASY	○ STINGY
○ SMOKEY	○ STINKY
○ CREAMY	○ SALTY

SAUCE

○ SWEET	○ SAVORY
○ TANGY	○ SPICY
○ THIN	○ CHUNKY

CHEESE TO SAUCE RATIO (CSR)

CHEESE	☐☐☐☐☐☐☐
SAUCE	☐☐☐☐☐☐☐

FRESHNESS

○1 ○2 ○3 ○4 ○5

CRUST SIZE

○ THIN
○ MEDIUM
○ LARGE

CRUST

○ BUTTERY	○ CRISPY
○ SPONGY	○ BUBBLY
○ CHEWY	○ OTHER

CRUST

○1 ○2 ○3 ○4 ○5

STYLE ○ NY ○ CHICAGO ○ OTHER

COMMENTS

MY RATING ○1 ○2 ○3 ○4 ○5 ○6 ○7 ○8 ○9 ○10

EAT AGAIN? ○ YES ○ NO

Pizza Log

DATE	
PIZZERIA	
NEIGHBORHOOD	

TOPPINGS		
○ CHEESE	○ MUSHROOMS	○ ONIONS
○ PINEAPPLE	○ BACON	○ TUNA
○ GREEN PEPPER	○ SAUSAGE	○ BLACK OLIVES
○ OTHER		

CHEESE	
○ GREASY	○ STINGY
○ SMOKEY	○ STINKY
○ CREAMY	○ SALTY

SAUCE	
○ SWEET	○ SAVORY
○ TANGY	○ SPICY
○ THIN	○ CHUNKY

CHEESE TO SAUCE RATIO (CSR)	
CHEESE	□□□□□□□
SAUCE	□□□□□□□

FRESHNESS

○1 ○2 ○3 ○4 ○5

CRUST SIZE	CRUST	
○ THIN	○ BUTTERY	○ CRISPY
○ MEDIUM	○ SPONGY	○ BUBBLY
○ LARGE	○ CHEWY	○ OTHER

CRUST

○1 ○2 ○3 ○4 ○5

STYLE	○ NY ○ CHICAGO ○ OTHER

COMMENTS

MY RATING	○1 ○2 ○3 ○4 ○5 ○6 ○7 ○8 ○9 ○10	EAT AGAIN?	○ YES ○ NO

Pizza Log

DATE	
PIZZERIA	
NEIGHBORHOOD	

TOPPINGS

O CHEESE	O MUSHROOMS	O ONIONS
O PINEAPPLE	O BACON	O TUNA
O GREEN PEPPER	O SAUSAGE	O BLACK OLIVES
O OTHER		

CHEESE

O GREASY	O STINGY
O SMOKEY	O STINKY
O CREAMY	O SALTY

SAUCE

O SWEET	O SAVORY
O TANGY	O SPICY
O THIN	O CHUNKY

CHEESE TO SAUCE RATIO (CSR)

CHEESE	□□□□□□□
SAUCE	□□□□□□□

FRESHNESS

O1 O2 O3 O4 O5

CRUST SIZE

O THIN
O MEDIUM
O LARGE

CRUST

O BUTTERY	O CRISPY
O SPONGY	O BUBBLY
O CHEWY	O OTHER

CRUST

O1 O2 O3 O4 O5

STYLE O NY O CHICAGO O OTHER

COMMENTS

MY RATING	O1 O2 O3 O4 O5 O6 O7 O8 O9 O10	EAT AGAIN?	O YES O NO

Pizza Log

DATE	
PIZZERIA	
NEIGHBORHOOD	

TOPPINGS

○ CHEESE	○ MUSHROOMS	○ ONIONS
○ PINEAPPLE	○ BACON	○ TUNA
○ GREEN PEPPER	○ SAUSAGE	○ BLACK OLIVES
○ OTHER		

CHEESE

○ GREASY	○ STINGY
○ SMOKEY	○ STINKY
○ CREAMY	○ SALTY

SAUCE

○ SWEET	○ SAVORY
○ TANGY	○ SPICY
○ THIN	○ CHUNKY

CHEESE TO SAUCE RATIO (CSR)

CHEESE	□□□□□□□
SAUCE	□□□□□□□

FRESHNESS

○1 ○2 ○3 ○4 ○5

CRUST SIZE

○ THIN
○ MEDIUM
○ LARGE

CRUST

○ BUTTERY	○ CRISPY
○ SPONGY	○ BUBBLY
○ CHEWY	○ OTHER

CRUST

○1 ○2 ○3 ○4 ○5

STYLE ○ NY ○ CHICAGO ○ OTHER

COMMENTS

MY RATING	○1 ○2 ○3 ○4 ○5 ○6 ○7 ○8 ○9 ○10	EAT AGAIN?	○ YES ○ NO

Pizza Log

DATE	
PIZZERIA	
NEIGHBORHOOD	

TOPPINGS		
○ CHEESE	○ MUSHROOMS	○ ONIONS
○ PINEAPPLE	○ BACON	○ TUNA
○ GREEN PEPPER	○ SAUSAGE	○ BLACK OLIVES
○ OTHER		

CHEESE	
○ GREASY	○ STINGY
○ SMOKEY	○ STINKY
○ CREAMY	○ SALTY

SAUCE	
○ SWEET	○ SAVORY
○ TANGY	○ SPICY
○ THIN	○ CHUNKY

FRESHNESS

○1 ○2 ○3 ○4 ○5

CHEESE TO SAUCE RATIO (CSR)	
CHEESE	□□□□□□□
SAUCE	□□□□□□□

CRUST SIZE	CRUST	
○ THIN	○ BUTTERY	○ CRISPY
○ MEDIUM	○ SPONGY	○ BUBBLY
○ LARGE	○ CHEWY	○ OTHER

CRUST

○1 ○2 ○3 ○4 ○5

STYLE	○ NY ○ CHICAGO ○ OTHER

COMMENTS

MY RATING	○1 ○2 ○3 ○4 ○5 ○6 ○7 ○8 ○9 ○10	EAT AGAIN?	○ YES ○ NO

Pizza Log

DATE	
PIZZERIA	
NEIGHBORHOOD	

TOPPINGS

○ CHEESE	○ MUSHROOMS	○ ONIONS
○ PINEAPPLE	○ BACON	○ TUNA
○ GREEN PEPPER	○ SAUSAGE	○ BLACK OLIVES
○ OTHER		

CHEESE

○ GREASY	○ STINGY
○ SMOKEY	○ STINKY
○ CREAMY	○ SALTY

SAUCE

○ SWEET	○ SAVORY
○ TANGY	○ SPICY
○ THIN	○ CHUNKY

CHEESE TO SAUCE RATIO (CSR)

CHEESE	☐☐☐☐☐☐☐
SAUCE	☐☐☐☐☐☐☐

FRESHNESS

○ 1 ○ 2 ○ 3 ○ 4 ○ 5

CRUST SIZE	CRUST	
○ THIN	○ BUTTERY	○ CRISPY
○ MEDIUM	○ SPONGY	○ BUBBLY
○ LARGE	○ CHEWY	○ OTHER

CRUST

○ 1 ○ 2 ○ 3 ○ 4 ○ 5

STYLE	○ NY ○ CHICAGO ○ OTHER

COMMENTS

MY RATING	○1 ○2 ○3 ○4 ○5 ○6 ○7 ○8 ○9 ○10	EAT AGAIN?	○ YES ○ NO

Pizza Log

DATE	
PIZZERIA	
NEIGHBORHOOD	

TOPPINGS		
○ CHEESE	○ MUSHROOMS	○ ONIONS
○ PINEAPPLE	○ BACON	○ TUNA
○ GREEN PEPPER	○ SAUSAGE	○ BLACK OLIVES
○ OTHER		

CHEESE	
○ GREASY	○ STINGY
○ SMOKEY	○ STINKY
○ CREAMY	○ SALTY

SAUCE	
○ SWEET	○ SAVORY
○ TANGY	○ SPICY
○ THIN	○ CHUNKY

CHEESE TO SAUCE RATIO (CSR)	
CHEESE	□ □ □ □ □ □ □
SAUCE	□ □ □ □ □ □ □

FRESHNESS

○ 1 ○ 2 ○ 3 ○ 4 ○ 5

CRUST SIZE	CRUST	
○ THIN	○ BUTTERY	○ CRISPY
○ MEDIUM	○ SPONGY	○ BUBBLY
○ LARGE	○ CHEWY	○ OTHER

CRUST

○ 1 ○ 2 ○ 3 ○ 4 ○ 5

STYLE	○ NY ○ CHICAGO ○ OTHER

COMMENTS

MY RATING	○1 ○2 ○3 ○4 ○5 ○6 ○7 ○8 ○9 ○10	EAT AGAIN?	○ YES ○ NO

Pizza Log

DATE	
PIZZERIA	
NEIGHBORHOOD	

TOPPINGS

○ CHEESE	○ MUSHROOMS	○ ONIONS
○ PINEAPPLE	○ BACON	○ TUNA
○ GREEN PEPPER	○ SAUSAGE	○ BLACK OLIVES

○ OTHER

CHEESE

○ GREASY	○ STINGY
○ SMOKEY	○ STINKY
○ CREAMY	○ SALTY

SAUCE

○ SWEET	○ SAVORY
○ TANGY	○ SPICY
○ THIN	○ CHUNKY

CHEESE TO SAUCE RATIO (CSR)

CHEESE	□□□□□□□
SAUCE	□□□□□□□

FRESHNESS

○1 ○2 ○3 ○4 ○5

CRUST SIZE

○ THIN
○ MEDIUM
○ LARGE

CRUST

○ BUTTERY	○ CRISPY
○ SPONGY	○ BUBBLY
○ CHEWY	○ OTHER

CRUST

○1 ○2 ○3 ○4 ○5

STYLE ○ NY ○ CHICAGO ○ OTHER

COMMENTS

MY RATING	○1 ○2 ○3 ○4 ○5 ○6 ○7 ○8 ○9 ○10	EAT AGAIN?	○ YES ○ NO

Pizza Log

DATE	
PIZZERIA	
NEIGHBORHOOD	

TOPPINGS		
○ CHEESE	○ MUSHROOMS	○ ONIONS
○ PINEAPPLE	○ BACON	○ TUNA
○ GREEN PEPPER	○ SAUSAGE	○ BLACK OLIVES
○ OTHER		

CHEESE	
○ GREASY	○ STINGY
○ SMOKEY	○ STINKY
○ CREAMY	○ SALTY

SAUCE	
○ SWEET	○ SAVORY
○ TANGY	○ SPICY
○ THIN	○ CHUNKY

CHEESE TO SAUCE RATIO (CSR)	
CHEESE	□□□□□□□
SAUCE	□□□□□□□

FRESHNESS

○1 ○2 ○3 ○4 ○5

CRUST SIZE	CRUST	
○ THIN	○ BUTTERY	○ CRISPY
○ MEDIUM	○ SPONGY	○ BUBBLY
○ LARGE	○ CHEWY	○ OTHER

CRUST

○1 ○2 ○3 ○4 ○5

STYLE	○ NY ○ CHICAGO ○ OTHER

COMMENTS

MY RATING	○1 ○2 ○3 ○4 ○5 ○6 ○7 ○8 ○9 ○10	EAT AGAIN?	○ YES ○ NO

Pizza Log

DATE	
PIZZERIA	
NEIGHBORHOOD	

TOPPINGS

○ CHEESE	○ MUSHROOMS	○ ONIONS
○ PINEAPPLE	○ BACON	○ TUNA
○ GREEN PEPPER	○ SAUSAGE	○ BLACK OLIVES

○ OTHER

CHEESE

○ GREASY	○ STINGY
○ SMOKEY	○ STINKY
○ CREAMY	○ SALTY

SAUCE

○ SWEET	○ SAVORY
○ TANGY	○ SPICY
○ THIN	○ CHUNKY

CHEESE TO SAUCE RATIO (CSR)

CHEESE	□□□□□□□
SAUCE	□□□□□□□

FRESHNESS

○1 ○2 ○3 ○4 ○5

CRUST SIZE

○ THIN
○ MEDIUM
○ LARGE

CRUST

○ BUTTERY	○ CRISPY
○ SPONGY	○ BUBBLY
○ CHEWY	○ OTHER

CRUST

○1 ○2 ○3 ○4 ○5

STYLE ○ NY ○ CHICAGO ○ OTHER

COMMENTS

MY RATING ○1 ○2 ○3 ○4 ○5 ○6 ○7 ○8 ○9 ○10

EAT AGAIN? ○ YES ○ NO

Pizza Log

DATE	
PIZZERIA	
NEIGHBORHOOD	

TOPPINGS

○ CHEESE	○ MUSHROOMS	○ ONIONS
○ PINEAPPLE	○ BACON	○ TUNA
○ GREEN PEPPER	○ SAUSAGE	○ BLACK OLIVES
○ OTHER		

CHEESE

○ GREASY	○ STINGY
○ SMOKEY	○ STINKY
○ CREAMY	○ SALTY

SAUCE

○ SWEET	○ SAVORY
○ TANGY	○ SPICY
○ THIN	○ CHUNKY

CHEESE TO SAUCE RATIO (CSR)

CHEESE	□□□□□□□
SAUCE	□□□□□□□

FRESHNESS

○1 ○2 ○3 ○4 ○5

CRUST SIZE

○ THIN
○ MEDIUM
○ LARGE

CRUST

○ BUTTERY	○ CRISPY
○ SPONGY	○ BUBBLY
○ CHEWY	○ OTHER

CRUST

○1 ○2 ○3 ○4 ○5

STYLE ○ NY ○ CHICAGO ○ OTHER

COMMENTS

MY RATING	○1 ○2 ○3 ○4 ○5 ○6 ○7 ○8 ○9 ○10	EAT AGAIN?	○ YES ○ NO

Pizza Log

DATE	
PIZZERIA	
NEIGHBORHOOD	

TOPPINGS		
○ CHEESE	○ MUSHROOMS	○ ONIONS
○ PINEAPPLE	○ BACON	○ TUNA
○ GREEN PEPPER	○ SAUSAGE	○ BLACK OLIVES
○ OTHER		

CHEESE	
○ GREASY	○ STINGY
○ SMOKEY	○ STINKY
○ CREAMY	○ SALTY

SAUCE	
○ SWEET	○ SAVORY
○ TANGY	○ SPICY
○ THIN	○ CHUNKY

CHEESE TO SAUCE RATIO (CSR)	
CHEESE	☐☐☐☐☐☐☐
SAUCE	☐☐☐☐☐☐☐

FRESHNESS

○1 ○2 ○3 ○4 ○5

CRUST SIZE	CRUST	
○ THIN	○ BUTTERY	○ CRISPY
○ MEDIUM	○ SPONGY	○ BUBBLY
○ LARGE	○ CHEWY	○ OTHER

CRUST

○1 ○2 ○3 ○4 ○5

STYLE	○ NY ○ CHICAGO ○ OTHER

COMMENTS

MY RATING	○1 ○2 ○3 ○4 ○5 ○6 ○7 ○8 ○9 ○10	EAT AGAIN?	○ YES ○ NO

Pizza Log

DATE	
PIZZERIA	
NEIGHBORHOOD	

TOPPINGS

○ CHEESE	○ MUSHROOMS	○ ONIONS
○ PINEAPPLE	○ BACON	○ TUNA
○ GREEN PEPPER	○ SAUSAGE	○ BLACK OLIVES
○ OTHER		

CHEESE

○ GREASY	○ STINGY
○ SMOKEY	○ STINKY
○ CREAMY	○ SALTY

SAUCE

○ SWEET	○ SAVORY
○ TANGY	○ SPICY
○ THIN	○ CHUNKY

CHEESE TO SAUCE RATIO (CSR)

CHEESE	□□□□□□□
SAUCE	□□□□□□□

FRESHNESS

○ 1 ○ 2 ○ 3 ○ 4 ○ 5

CRUST SIZE

○ THIN
○ MEDIUM
○ LARGE

CRUST

○ BUTTERY	○ CRISPY
○ SPONGY	○ BUBBLY
○ CHEWY	○ OTHER

CRUST

○ 1 ○ 2 ○ 3 ○ 4 ○ 5

STYLE	○ NY ○ CHICAGO ○ OTHER

COMMENTS

MY RATING	○1 ○2 ○3 ○4 ○5 ○6 ○7 ○8 ○9 ○10	EAT AGAIN?	○ YES ○ NO

Pizza Log

DATE	
PIZZERIA	
NEIGHBORHOOD	

TOPPINGS		
○ CHEESE	○ MUSHROOMS	○ ONIONS
○ PINEAPPLE	○ BACON	○ TUNA
○ GREEN PEPPER	○ SAUSAGE	○ BLACK OLIVES
○ OTHER		

CHEESE	
○ GREASY	○ STINGY
○ SMOKEY	○ STINKY
○ CREAMY	○ SALTY

SAUCE	
○ SWEET	○ SAVORY
○ TANGY	○ SPICY
○ THIN	○ CHUNKY

CHEESE TO SAUCE RATIO (CSR)	
CHEESE	☐☐☐☐☐☐☐
SAUCE	☐☐☐☐☐☐☐

FRESHNESS

○1 ○2 ○3 ○4 ○5

CRUST SIZE	CRUST	
○ THIN	○ BUTTERY	○ CRISPY
○ MEDIUM	○ SPONGY	○ BUBBLY
○ LARGE	○ CHEWY	○ OTHER

CRUST

○1 ○2 ○3 ○4 ○5

STYLE	○ NY ○ CHICAGO ○ OTHER

COMMENTS

MY RATING	○1 ○2 ○3 ○4 ○5 ○6 ○7 ○8 ○9 ○10	EAT AGAIN?	○ YES ○ NO

Pizza Log

DATE	
PIZZERIA	
NEIGHBORHOOD	

TOPPINGS

○ CHEESE	○ MUSHROOMS	○ ONIONS
○ PINEAPPLE	○ BACON	○ TUNA
○ GREEN PEPPER	○ SAUSAGE	○ BLACK OLIVES
○ OTHER		

CHEESE

○ GREASY	○ STINGY
○ SMOKEY	○ STINKY
○ CREAMY	○ SALTY

SAUCE

○ SWEET	○ SAVORY
○ TANGY	○ SPICY
○ THIN	○ CHUNKY

CHEESE TO SAUCE RATIO (CSR)

CHEESE	☐☐☐☐☐☐☐
SAUCE	☐☐☐☐☐☐☐

FRESHNESS

○1 ○2 ○3 ○4 ○5

CRUST SIZE	CRUST	
○ THIN	○ BUTTERY	○ CRISPY
○ MEDIUM	○ SPONGY	○ BUBBLY
○ LARGE	○ CHEWY	○ OTHER

CRUST

○1 ○2 ○3 ○4 ○5

STYLE ○ NY ○ CHICAGO ○ OTHER

COMMENTS

MY RATING	○1 ○2 ○3 ○4 ○5 ○6 ○7 ○8 ○9 ○10	EAT AGAIN?	○ YES ○ NO

Pizza Log

DATE	
PIZZERIA	
NEIGHBORHOOD	

TOPPINGS

O CHEESE	O MUSHROOMS	O ONIONS
O PINEAPPLE	O BACON	O TUNA
O GREEN PEPPER	O SAUSAGE	O BLACK OLIVES
O OTHER		

CHEESE

O GREASY	O STINGY
O SMOKEY	O STINKY
O CREAMY	O SALTY

SAUCE

O SWEET	O SAVORY
O TANGY	O SPICY
O THIN	O CHUNKY

CHEESE TO SAUCE RATIO (CSR)

CHEESE	☐☐☐☐☐☐☐
SAUCE	☐☐☐☐☐☐☐

FRESHNESS

O1 O2 O3 O4 O5

CRUST SIZE

O THIN
O MEDIUM
O LARGE

CRUST

O BUTTERY	O CRISPY
O SPONGY	O BUBBLY
O CHEWY	O OTHER

CRUST

O1 O2 O3 O4 O5

STYLE O NY O CHICAGO O OTHER

COMMENTS

MY RATING	O1 O2 O3 O4 O5 O6 O7 O8 O9 O10	EAT AGAIN?	O YES O NO

Pizza Log

DATE	
PIZZERIA	
NEIGHBORHOOD	

TOPPINGS

○ CHEESE	○ MUSHROOMS	○ ONIONS
○ PINEAPPLE	○ BACON	○ TUNA
○ GREEN PEPPER	○ SAUSAGE	○ BLACK OLIVES
○ OTHER		

CHEESE

○ GREASY	○ STINGY
○ SMOKEY	○ STINKY
○ CREAMY	○ SALTY

SAUCE

○ SWEET	○ SAVORY
○ TANGY	○ SPICY
○ THIN	○ CHUNKY

FRESHNESS

○ 1 ○ 2 ○ 3 ○ 4 ○ 5

CHEESE TO SAUCE RATIO (CSR)

CHEESE	□□□□□□□
SAUCE	□□□□□□□

CRUST SIZE

○ THIN
○ MEDIUM
○ LARGE

CRUST

○ BUTTERY	○ CRISPY
○ SPONGY	○ BUBBLY
○ CHEWY	○ OTHER

CRUST

○ 1 ○ 2 ○ 3 ○ 4 ○ 5

STYLE ○ NY ○ CHICAGO ○ OTHER

COMMENTS

MY RATING ○1 ○2 ○3 ○4 ○5 ○6 ○7 ○8 ○9 ○10

EAT AGAIN? ○ YES ○ NO

Pizza Log

DATE	
PIZZERIA	
NEIGHBORHOOD	

TOPPINGS

○ CHEESE	○ MUSHROOMS	○ ONIONS
○ PINEAPPLE	○ BACON	○ TUNA
○ GREEN PEPPER	○ SAUSAGE	○ BLACK OLIVES

○ OTHER

CHEESE

○ GREASY	○ STINGY
○ SMOKEY	○ STINKY
○ CREAMY	○ SALTY

SAUCE

○ SWEET	○ SAVORY
○ TANGY	○ SPICY
○ THIN	○ CHUNKY

CHEESE TO SAUCE RATIO (CSR)

CHEESE	☐ ☐ ☐ ☐ ☐ ☐ ☐
SAUCE	☐ ☐ ☐ ☐ ☐ ☐ ☐

FRESHNESS

○ 1 ○ 2 ○ 3 ○ 4 ○ 5

CRUST SIZE	CRUST	
○ THIN	○ BUTTERY	○ CRISPY
○ MEDIUM	○ SPONGY	○ BUBBLY
○ LARGE	○ CHEWY	○ OTHER

CRUST

○ 1 ○ 2 ○ 3 ○ 4 ○ 5

STYLE ○ NY ○ CHICAGO ○ OTHER

COMMENTS

MY RATING	○ 1 ○ 2 ○ 3 ○ 4 ○ 5 ○ 6 ○ 7 ○ 8 ○ 9 ○ 10	EAT AGAIN?	○ YES ○ NO

Pizza Log

DATE	
PIZZERIA	
NEIGHBORHOOD	

TOPPINGS		
○ CHEESE	○ MUSHROOMS	○ ONIONS
○ PINEAPPLE	○ BACON	○ TUNA
○ GREEN PEPPER	○ SAUSAGE	○ BLACK OLIVES
○ OTHER		

CHEESE	
○ GREASY	○ STINGY
○ SMOKEY	○ STINKY
○ CREAMY	○ SALTY

SAUCE	
○ SWEET	○ SAVORY
○ TANGY	○ SPICY
○ THIN	○ CHUNKY

CHEESE TO SAUCE RATIO (CSR)	
CHEESE	□□□□□□□
SAUCE	□□□□□□□

FRESHNESS

○1 ○2 ○3 ○4 ○5

CRUST SIZE	CRUST	
○ THIN	○ BUTTERY	○ CRISPY
○ MEDIUM	○ SPONGY	○ BUBBLY
○ LARGE	○ CHEWY	○ OTHER

CRUST

○1 ○2 ○3 ○4 ○5

STYLE	○ NY ○ CHICAGO ○ OTHER

COMMENTS

MY RATING	○1 ○2 ○3 ○4 ○5 ○6 ○7 ○8 ○9 ○10	EAT AGAIN?	○ YES ○ NO

Pizza Log

DATE	
PIZZERIA	
NEIGHBORHOOD	

TOPPINGS

○ CHEESE	○ MUSHROOMS	○ ONIONS
○ PINEAPPLE	○ BACON	○ TUNA
○ GREEN PEPPER	○ SAUSAGE	○ BLACK OLIVES
○ OTHER		

CHEESE

○ GREASY	○ STINGY
○ SMOKEY	○ STINKY
○ CREAMY	○ SALTY

SAUCE

○ SWEET	○ SAVORY
○ TANGY	○ SPICY
○ THIN	○ CHUNKY

CHEESE TO SAUCE RATIO (CSR)

CHEESE	☐☐☐☐☐☐☐
SAUCE	☐☐☐☐☐☐☐

FRESHNESS

○1 ○2 ○3 ○4 ○5

CRUST SIZE

○ THIN
○ MEDIUM
○ LARGE

CRUST

○ BUTTERY	○ CRISPY
○ SPONGY	○ BUBBLY
○ CHEWY	○ OTHER

CRUST

○1 ○2 ○3 ○4 ○5

STYLE ○ NY ○ CHICAGO ○ OTHER

COMMENTS

MY RATING	○1 ○2 ○3 ○4 ○5 ○6 ○7 ○8 ○9 ○10	EAT AGAIN?	○ YES ○ NO

Pizza Log

DATE	
PIZZERIA	
NEIGHBORHOOD	

TOPPINGS

○ CHEESE	○ MUSHROOMS	○ ONIONS
○ PINEAPPLE	○ BACON	○ TUNA
○ GREEN PEPPER	○ SAUSAGE	○ BLACK OLIVES
○ OTHER		

CHEESE

○ GREASY	○ STINGY
○ SMOKEY	○ STINKY
○ CREAMY	○ SALTY

SAUCE

○ SWEET	○ SAVORY
○ TANGY	○ SPICY
○ THIN	○ CHUNKY

CHEESE TO SAUCE RATIO (CSR)

CHEESE	□ □ □ □ □ □ □
SAUCE	□ □ □ □ □ □ □

FRESHNESS

○1 ○2 ○3 ○4 ○5

CRUST SIZE

○ THIN
○ MEDIUM
○ LARGE

CRUST

○ BUTTERY	○ CRISPY
○ SPONGY	○ BUBBLY
○ CHEWY	○ OTHER

CRUST

○1 ○2 ○3 ○4 ○5

STYLE ○ NY ○ CHICAGO ○ OTHER

COMMENTS

MY RATING ○1 ○2 ○3 ○4 ○5 ○6 ○7 ○8 ○9 ○10

EAT AGAIN? ○ YES ○ NO

Pizza Log

DATE	
PIZZERIA	
NEIGHBORHOOD	

TOPPINGS

○ CHEESE	○ MUSHROOMS	○ ONIONS
○ PINEAPPLE	○ BACON	○ TUNA
○ GREEN PEPPER	○ SAUSAGE	○ BLACK OLIVES
○ OTHER		

CHEESE

○ GREASY	○ STINGY
○ SMOKEY	○ STINKY
○ CREAMY	○ SALTY

SAUCE

○ SWEET	○ SAVORY
○ TANGY	○ SPICY
○ THIN	○ CHUNKY

CHEESE TO SAUCE RATIO (CSR)

CHEESE	□ □ □ □ □ □ □
SAUCE	□ □ □ □ □ □ □

FRESHNESS

○1 ○2 ○3 ○4 ○5

CRUST SIZE

○ THIN
○ MEDIUM
○ LARGE

CRUST

○ BUTTERY	○ CRISPY
○ SPONGY	○ BUBBLY
○ CHEWY	○ OTHER

CRUST

○1 ○2 ○3 ○4 ○5

STYLE	○ NY ○ CHICAGO ○ OTHER

COMMENTS

MY RATING	○1 ○2 ○3 ○4 ○5 ○6 ○7 ○8 ○9 ○10	EAT AGAIN?	○ YES ○ NO

Pizza Log

DATE	
PIZZERIA	
NEIGHBORHOOD	

TOPPINGS

O CHEESE	O MUSHROOMS	O ONIONS
O PINEAPPLE	O BACON	O TUNA
O GREEN PEPPER	O SAUSAGE	O BLACK OLIVES
O OTHER		

CHEESE

O GREASY	O STINGY
O SMOKEY	O STINKY
O CREAMY	O SALTY

SAUCE

O SWEET	O SAVORY
O TANGY	O SPICY
O THIN	O CHUNKY

CHEESE TO SAUCE RATIO (CSR)

CHEESE	□ □ □ □ □ □ □
SAUCE	□ □ □ □ □ □ □

FRESHNESS

O1 O2 O3 O4 O5

CRUST SIZE

O THIN
O MEDIUM
O LARGE

CRUST

O BUTTERY	O CRISPY
O SPONGY	O BUBBLY
O CHEWY	O OTHER

CRUST

O1 O2 O3 O4 O5

STYLE O NY O CHICAGO O OTHER

COMMENTS

MY RATING O1 O2 O3 O4 O5 O6 O7 O8 O9 O10

EAT AGAIN? O YES O NO

Pizza Log

DATE	
PIZZERIA	
NEIGHBORHOOD	

TOPPINGS

○ CHEESE	○ MUSHROOMS	○ ONIONS
○ PINEAPPLE	○ BACON	○ TUNA
○ GREEN PEPPER	○ SAUSAGE	○ BLACK OLIVES
○ OTHER		

CHEESE

○ GREASY	○ STINGY
○ SMOKEY	○ STINKY
○ CREAMY	○ SALTY

SAUCE

○ SWEET	○ SAVORY
○ TANGY	○ SPICY
○ THIN	○ CHUNKY

CHEESE TO SAUCE RATIO (CSR)

CHEESE	☐☐☐☐☐☐☐
SAUCE	☐☐☐☐☐☐☐

FRESHNESS

○1 ○2 ○3 ○4 ○5

CRUST SIZE

○ THIN
○ MEDIUM
○ LARGE

CRUST

○ BUTTERY	○ CRISPY
○ SPONGY	○ BUBBLY
○ CHEWY	○ OTHER

CRUST

○1 ○2 ○3 ○4 ○5

STYLE ○ NY ○ CHICAGO ○ OTHER

COMMENTS

MY RATING ○1 ○2 ○3 ○4 ○5 ○6 ○7 ○8 ○9 ○10

EAT AGAIN? ○ YES ○ NO

Pizza Log

DATE	
PIZZERIA	
NEIGHBORHOOD	

TOPPINGS		
○ CHEESE	○ MUSHROOMS	○ ONIONS
○ PINEAPPLE	○ BACON	○ TUNA
○ GREEN PEPPER	○ SAUSAGE	○ BLACK OLIVES
○ OTHER		

CHEESE	
○ GREASY	○ STINGY
○ SMOKEY	○ STINKY
○ CREAMY	○ SALTY

SAUCE	
○ SWEET	○ SAVORY
○ TANGY	○ SPICY
○ THIN	○ CHUNKY

CHEESE TO SAUCE RATIO (CSR)	
CHEESE	☐☐☐☐☐☐☐
SAUCE	☐☐☐☐☐☐☐

FRESHNESS

○1 ○2 ○3 ○4 ○5

CRUST SIZE	CRUST	
○ THIN	○ BUTTERY	○ CRISPY
○ MEDIUM	○ SPONGY	○ BUBBLY
○ LARGE	○ CHEWY	○ OTHER

CRUST

○1 ○2 ○3 ○4 ○5

STYLE	○ NY ○ CHICAGO ○ OTHER

COMMENTS

MY RATING	○1 ○2 ○3 ○4 ○5 ○6 ○7 ○8 ○9 ○10	EAT AGAIN?	○ YES ○ NO

Pizza Log

DATE	
PIZZERIA	
NEIGHBORHOOD	

TOPPINGS

○ CHEESE	○ MUSHROOMS	○ ONIONS
○ PINEAPPLE	○ BACON	○ TUNA
○ GREEN PEPPER	○ SAUSAGE	○ BLACK OLIVES
○ OTHER		

CHEESE

○ GREASY	○ STINGY
○ SMOKEY	○ STINKY
○ CREAMY	○ SALTY

SAUCE

○ SWEET	○ SAVORY
○ TANGY	○ SPICY
○ THIN	○ CHUNKY

CHEESE TO SAUCE RATIO (CSR)

CHEESE	□□□□□□□
SAUCE	□□□□□□□

FRESHNESS

○1 ○2 ○3 ○4 ○5

CRUST SIZE

○ THIN
○ MEDIUM
○ LARGE

CRUST

○ BUTTERY	○ CRISPY
○ SPONGY	○ BUBBLY
○ CHEWY	○ OTHER

CRUST

○1 ○2 ○3 ○4 ○5

STYLE ○ NY ○ CHICAGO ○ OTHER

COMMENTS

MY RATING	○1 ○2 ○3 ○4 ○5 ○6 ○7 ○8 ○9 ○10	EAT AGAIN?	○ YES ○ NO

Pizza Log

DATE	
PIZZERIA	
NEIGHBORHOOD	

TOPPINGS

○ CHEESE	○ MUSHROOMS	○ ONIONS
○ PINEAPPLE	○ BACON	○ TUNA
○ GREEN PEPPER	○ SAUSAGE	○ BLACK OLIVES
○ OTHER		

CHEESE

○ GREASY	○ STINGY
○ SMOKEY	○ STINKY
○ CREAMY	○ SALTY

SAUCE

○ SWEET	○ SAVORY
○ TANGY	○ SPICY
○ THIN	○ CHUNKY

CHEESE TO SAUCE RATIO (CSR)

CHEESE	□□□□□□□
SAUCE	□□□□□□□

FRESHNESS

○1 ○2 ○3 ○4 ○5

CRUST SIZE

○ THIN
○ MEDIUM
○ LARGE

CRUST

○ BUTTERY	○ CRISPY
○ SPONGY	○ BUBBLY
○ CHEWY	○ OTHER

CRUST

○1 ○2 ○3 ○4 ○5

STYLE ○ NY ○ CHICAGO ○ OTHER

COMMENTS

MY RATING	○1 ○2 ○3 ○4 ○5 ○6 ○7 ○8 ○9 ○10	EAT AGAIN?	○ YES ○ NO

Pizza Log

DATE	
PIZZERIA	
NEIGHBORHOOD	

TOPPINGS		
○ CHEESE	○ MUSHROOMS	○ ONIONS
○ PINEAPPLE	○ BACON	○ TUNA
○ GREEN PEPPER	○ SAUSAGE	○ BLACK OLIVES
○ OTHER		

CHEESE	
○ GREASY	○ STINGY
○ SMOKEY	○ STINKY
○ CREAMY	○ SALTY

SAUCE	
○ SWEET	○ SAVORY
○ TANGY	○ SPICY
○ THIN	○ CHUNKY

CHEESE TO SAUCE RATIO (CSR)	
CHEESE	□□□□□□□
SAUCE	□□□□□□□

FRESHNESS

○1 ○2 ○3 ○4 ○5

CRUST SIZE	CRUST	
○ THIN	○ BUTTERY	○ CRISPY
○ MEDIUM	○ SPONGY	○ BUBBLY
○ LARGE	○ CHEWY	○ OTHER

CRUST

○1 ○2 ○3 ○4 ○5

STYLE	○ NY ○ CHICAGO ○ OTHER

COMMENTS

MY RATING	○1 ○2 ○3 ○4 ○5 ○6 ○7 ○8 ○9 ○10	EAT AGAIN?	○ YES ○ NO

Pizza Log

DATE	
PIZZERIA	
NEIGHBORHOOD	

TOPPINGS		
O CHEESE	O MUSHROOMS	O ONIONS
O PINEAPPLE	O BACON	O TUNA
O GREEN PEPPER	O SAUSAGE	O BLACK OLIVES
O OTHER		

CHEESE	
O GREASY	O STINGY
O SMOKEY	O STINKY
O CREAMY	O SALTY

SAUCE	
O SWEET	O SAVORY
O TANGY	O SPICY
O THIN	O CHUNKY

FRESHNESS

O1 O2 O3 O4 O5

CHEESE TO SAUCE RATIO (CSR)	
CHEESE	□□□□□□□
SAUCE	□□□□□□□

CRUST SIZE	CRUST	
O THIN	O BUTTERY	O CRISPY
O MEDIUM	O SPONGY	O BUBBLY
O LARGE	O CHEWY	O OTHER

CRUST

O1 O2 O3 O4 O5

STYLE	O NY O CHICAGO O OTHER

COMMENTS

MY RATING	O1 O2 O3 O4 O5 O6 O7 O8 O9 O10	EAT AGAIN?	O YES O NO

Pizza Log

DATE	
PIZZERIA	
NEIGHBORHOOD	

TOPPINGS

○ CHEESE	○ MUSHROOMS	○ ONIONS
○ PINEAPPLE	○ BACON	○ TUNA
○ GREEN PEPPER	○ SAUSAGE	○ BLACK OLIVES
○ OTHER		

CHEESE

○ GREASY	○ STINGY
○ SMOKEY	○ STINKY
○ CREAMY	○ SALTY

SAUCE

○ SWEET	○ SAVORY
○ TANGY	○ SPICY
○ THIN	○ CHUNKY

CHEESE TO SAUCE RATIO (CSR)

CHEESE	☐☐☐☐☐☐☐
SAUCE	☐☐☐☐☐☐☐

FRESHNESS

○1 ○2 ○3 ○4 ○5

CRUST SIZE

○ THIN
○ MEDIUM
○ LARGE

CRUST

○ BUTTERY	○ CRISPY
○ SPONGY	○ BUBBLY
○ CHEWY	○ OTHER

CRUST

○1 ○2 ○3 ○4 ○5

STYLE ○ NY ○ CHICAGO ○ OTHER

COMMENTS

MY RATING	○1 ○2 ○3 ○4 ○5 ○6 ○7 ○8 ○9 ○10	EAT AGAIN?	○ YES ○ NO

Pizza Log

DATE	
PIZZERIA	
NEIGHBORHOOD	

TOPPINGS		
○ CHEESE	○ MUSHROOMS	○ ONIONS
○ PINEAPPLE	○ BACON	○ TUNA
○ GREEN PEPPER	○ SAUSAGE	○ BLACK OLIVES
○ OTHER		

CHEESE	
○ GREASY	○ STINGY
○ SMOKEY	○ STINKY
○ CREAMY	○ SALTY

SAUCE	
○ SWEET	○ SAVORY
○ TANGY	○ SPICY
○ THIN	○ CHUNKY

CHEESE TO SAUCE RATIO (CSR)	
CHEESE	□ □ □ □ □ □ □
SAUCE	□ □ □ □ □ □ □

FRESHNESS

○ 1 ○ 2 ○ 3 ○ 4 ○ 5

CRUST SIZE	CRUST	
○ THIN	○ BUTTERY	○ CRISPY
○ MEDIUM	○ SPONGY	○ BUBBLY
○ LARGE	○ CHEWY	○ OTHER

CRUST

○ 1 ○ 2 ○ 3 ○ 4 ○ 5

STYLE	○ NY ○ CHICAGO ○ OTHER

COMMENTS

MY RATING	○1 ○2 ○3 ○4 ○5 ○6 ○7 ○8 ○9 ○10	EAT AGAIN?	○ YES ○ NO

Pizza Log

DATE	
PIZZERIA	
NEIGHBORHOOD	

TOPPINGS		
○ CHEESE	○ MUSHROOMS	○ ONIONS
○ PINEAPPLE	○ BACON	○ TUNA
○ GREEN PEPPER	○ SAUSAGE	○ BLACK OLIVES
○ OTHER		

CHEESE	
○ GREASY	○ STINGY
○ SMOKEY	○ STINKY
○ CREAMY	○ SALTY

SAUCE	
○ SWEET	○ SAVORY
○ TANGY	○ SPICY
○ THIN	○ CHUNKY

CHEESE TO SAUCE RATIO (CSR)	
CHEESE	☐ ☐ ☐ ☐ ☐ ☐ ☐
SAUCE	☐ ☐ ☐ ☐ ☐ ☐ ☐

FRESHNESS

○ 1 ○ 2 ○ 3 ○ 4 ○ 5

CRUST SIZE	CRUST	
○ THIN	○ BUTTERY	○ CRISPY
○ MEDIUM	○ SPONGY	○ BUBBLY
○ LARGE	○ CHEWY	○ OTHER

CRUST

○ 1 ○ 2 ○ 3 ○ 4 ○ 5

STYLE	○ NY ○ CHICAGO ○ OTHER

COMMENTS

MY RATING	○1 ○2 ○3 ○4 ○5 ○6 ○7 ○8 ○9 ○10	EAT AGAIN?	○ YES ○ NO

Pizza Log

DATE	
PIZZERIA	
NEIGHBORHOOD	

TOPPINGS

○ CHEESE	○ MUSHROOMS	○ ONIONS
○ PINEAPPLE	○ BACON	○ TUNA
○ GREEN PEPPER	○ SAUSAGE	○ BLACK OLIVES
○ OTHER		

CHEESE

○ GREASY	○ STINGY
○ SMOKEY	○ STINKY
○ CREAMY	○ SALTY

SAUCE

○ SWEET	○ SAVORY
○ TANGY	○ SPICY
○ THIN	○ CHUNKY

CHEESE TO SAUCE RATIO (CSR)

CHEESE	□□□□□□□
SAUCE	□□□□□□□

FRESHNESS

○1 ○2 ○3 ○4 ○5

CRUST SIZE

○ THIN
○ MEDIUM
○ LARGE

CRUST

○ BUTTERY	○ CRISPY
○ SPONGY	○ BUBBLY
○ CHEWY	○ OTHER

CRUST

○1 ○2 ○3 ○4 ○5

STYLE ○ NY ○ CHICAGO ○ OTHER

COMMENTS

MY RATING ○1 ○2 ○3 ○4 ○5 ○6 ○7 ○8 ○9 ○10

EAT AGAIN? ○ YES ○ NO

Pizza Log

DATE	
PIZZERIA	
NEIGHBORHOOD	

TOPPINGS		
○ CHEESE	○ MUSHROOMS	○ ONIONS
○ PINEAPPLE	○ BACON	○ TUNA
○ GREEN PEPPER	○ SAUSAGE	○ BLACK OLIVES
○ OTHER		

CHEESE	
○ GREASY	○ STINGY
○ SMOKEY	○ STINKY
○ CREAMY	○ SALTY

SAUCE	
○ SWEET	○ SAVORY
○ TANGY	○ SPICY
○ THIN	○ CHUNKY

CHEESE TO SAUCE RATIO (CSR)	
CHEESE	☐☐☐☐☐☐☐
SAUCE	☐☐☐☐☐☐☐

FRESHNESS

○1 ○2 ○3 ○4 ○5

CRUST SIZE	CRUST	
○ THIN	○ BUTTERY	○ CRISPY
○ MEDIUM	○ SPONGY	○ BUBBLY
○ LARGE	○ CHEWY	○ OTHER

CRUST

○1 ○2 ○3 ○4 ○5

STYLE	○ NY ○ CHICAGO ○ OTHER

COMMENTS

MY RATING	○1 ○2 ○3 ○4 ○5 ○6 ○7 ○8 ○9 ○10	EAT AGAIN?	○ YES ○ NO

Pizza Log

DATE	
PIZZERIA	
NEIGHBORHOOD	

TOPPINGS

- ○ CHEESE
- ○ MUSHROOMS
- ○ ONIONS
- ○ PINEAPPLE
- ○ BACON
- ○ TUNA
- ○ GREEN PEPPER
- ○ SAUSAGE
- ○ BLACK OLIVES
- ○ OTHER

CHEESE

- ○ GREASY
- ○ STINGY
- ○ SMOKEY
- ○ STINKY
- ○ CREAMY
- ○ SALTY

SAUCE

- ○ SWEET
- ○ SAVORY
- ○ TANGY
- ○ SPICY
- ○ THIN
- ○ CHUNKY

FRESHNESS

○1 ○2 ○3 ○4 ○5

CHEESE TO SAUCE RATIO (CSR)

CHEESE	□□□□□□□
SAUCE	□□□□□□□

CRUST SIZE

- ○ THIN
- ○ MEDIUM
- ○ LARGE

CRUST

- ○ BUTTERY
- ○ CRISPY
- ○ SPONGY
- ○ BUBBLY
- ○ CHEWY
- ○ OTHER

CRUST

○1 ○2 ○3 ○4 ○5

STYLE ○ NY ○ CHICAGO ○ OTHER

COMMENTS

MY RATING ○1 ○2 ○3 ○4 ○5 ○6 ○7 ○8 ○9 ○10

EAT AGAIN? ○ YES ○ NO

Pizza Log

DATE	
PIZZERIA	
NEIGHBORHOOD	

TOPPINGS

○ CHEESE	○ MUSHROOMS	○ ONIONS
○ PINEAPPLE	○ BACON	○ TUNA
○ GREEN PEPPER	○ SAUSAGE	○ BLACK OLIVES
○ OTHER		

CHEESE

○ GREASY	○ STINGY
○ SMOKEY	○ STINKY
○ CREAMY	○ SALTY

SAUCE

○ SWEET	○ SAVORY
○ TANGY	○ SPICY
○ THIN	○ CHUNKY

CHEESE TO SAUCE RATIO (CSR)

CHEESE	☐☐☐☐☐☐☐
SAUCE	☐☐☐☐☐☐☐

FRESHNESS

○1 ○2 ○3 ○4 ○5

CRUST SIZE

○ THIN
○ MEDIUM
○ LARGE

CRUST

○ BUTTERY	○ CRISPY
○ SPONGY	○ BUBBLY
○ CHEWY	○ OTHER

CRUST

○1 ○2 ○3 ○4 ○5

STYLE ○ NY ○ CHICAGO ○ OTHER

COMMENTS

MY RATING	○1 ○2 ○3 ○4 ○5 ○6 ○7 ○8 ○9 ○10	EAT AGAIN?	○ YES ○ NO

Pizza Log

DATE	
PIZZERIA	
NEIGHBORHOOD	

TOPPINGS

○ CHEESE	○ MUSHROOMS	○ ONIONS
○ PINEAPPLE	○ BACON	○ TUNA
○ GREEN PEPPER	○ SAUSAGE	○ BLACK OLIVES
○ OTHER		

CHEESE

○ GREASY	○ STINGY
○ SMOKEY	○ STINKY
○ CREAMY	○ SALTY

SAUCE

○ SWEET	○ SAVORY
○ TANGY	○ SPICY
○ THIN	○ CHUNKY

CHEESE TO SAUCE RATIO (CSR)

CHEESE	☐☐☐☐☐☐☐
SAUCE	☐☐☐☐☐☐☐

FRESHNESS

○1 ○2 ○3 ○4 ○5

CRUST SIZE

○ THIN
○ MEDIUM
○ LARGE

CRUST

○ BUTTERY	○ CRISPY
○ SPONGY	○ BUBBLY
○ CHEWY	○ OTHER

CRUST

○1 ○2 ○3 ○4 ○5

STYLE ○ NY ○ CHICAGO ○ OTHER

COMMENTS

MY RATING ○1 ○2 ○3 ○4 ○5 ○6 ○7 ○8 ○9 ○10

EAT AGAIN? ○ YES ○ NO

Pizza Log

DATE	
PIZZERIA	
NEIGHBORHOOD	

TOPPINGS

○ CHEESE	○ MUSHROOMS	○ ONIONS
○ PINEAPPLE	○ BACON	○ TUNA
○ GREEN PEPPER	○ SAUSAGE	○ BLACK OLIVES

○ OTHER

CHEESE

○ GREASY	○ STINGY
○ SMOKEY	○ STINKY
○ CREAMY	○ SALTY

SAUCE

○ SWEET	○ SAVORY
○ TANGY	○ SPICY
○ THIN	○ CHUNKY

CHEESE TO SAUCE RATIO (CSR)

CHEESE	□□□□□□□
SAUCE	□□□□□□□

FRESHNESS

○ 1 ○ 2 ○ 3 ○ 4 ○ 5

CRUST SIZE

○ THIN
○ MEDIUM
○ LARGE

CRUST

○ BUTTERY	○ CRISPY
○ SPONGY	○ BUBBLY
○ CHEWY	○ OTHER

CRUST

○ 1 ○ 2 ○ 3 ○ 4 ○ 5

STYLE ○ NY ○ CHICAGO ○ OTHER

COMMENTS

MY RATING	○1 ○2 ○3 ○4 ○5 ○6 ○7 ○8 ○9 ○10	EAT AGAIN?	○ YES ○ NO

Pizza Log

DATE	
PIZZERIA	
NEIGHBORHOOD	

TOPPINGS

○ CHEESE	○ MUSHROOMS	○ ONIONS
○ PINEAPPLE	○ BACON	○ TUNA
○ GREEN PEPPER	○ SAUSAGE	○ BLACK OLIVES
○ OTHER		

CHEESE

○ GREASY	○ STINGY
○ SMOKEY	○ STINKY
○ CREAMY	○ SALTY

SAUCE

○ SWEET	○ SAVORY
○ TANGY	○ SPICY
○ THIN	○ CHUNKY

CHEESE TO SAUCE RATIO (CSR)

CHEESE	□□□□□□□
SAUCE	□□□□□□□

FRESHNESS

○1 ○2 ○3 ○4 ○5

CRUST SIZE

○ THIN
○ MEDIUM
○ LARGE

CRUST

○ BUTTERY	○ CRISPY
○ SPONGY	○ BUBBLY
○ CHEWY	○ OTHER

CRUST

○1 ○2 ○3 ○4 ○5

STYLE ○ NY ○ CHICAGO ○ OTHER

COMMENTS

MY RATING ○1 ○2 ○3 ○4 ○5 ○6 ○7 ○8 ○9 ○10

EAT AGAIN? ○ YES ○ NO

Pizza Log

DATE	
PIZZERIA	
NEIGHBORHOOD	

TOPPINGS

○ CHEESE	○ MUSHROOMS	○ ONIONS
○ PINEAPPLE	○ BACON	○ TUNA
○ GREEN PEPPER	○ SAUSAGE	○ BLACK OLIVES
○ OTHER		

CHEESE

○ GREASY	○ STINGY
○ SMOKEY	○ STINKY
○ CREAMY	○ SALTY

SAUCE

○ SWEET	○ SAVORY
○ TANGY	○ SPICY
○ THIN	○ CHUNKY

CHEESE TO SAUCE RATIO (CSR)

CHEESE	☐ ☐ ☐ ☐ ☐ ☐ ☐
SAUCE	☐ ☐ ☐ ☐ ☐ ☐ ☐

FRESHNESS

○ 1 ○ 2 ○ 3 ○ 4 ○ 5

CRUST SIZE

○ THIN
○ MEDIUM
○ LARGE

CRUST

○ BUTTERY	○ CRISPY
○ SPONGY	○ BUBBLY
○ CHEWY	○ OTHER

CRUST

○ 1 ○ 2 ○ 3 ○ 4 ○ 5

STYLE ○ NY ○ CHICAGO ○ OTHER

COMMENTS

MY RATING ○ 1 ○ 2 ○ 3 ○ 4 ○ 5 ○ 6 ○ 7 ○ 8 ○ 9 ○ 10

EAT AGAIN? ○ YES ○ NO

Pizza Log

DATE	
PIZZERIA	
NEIGHBORHOOD	

TOPPINGS

○ CHEESE	○ MUSHROOMS	○ ONIONS
○ PINEAPPLE	○ BACON	○ TUNA
○ GREEN PEPPER	○ SAUSAGE	○ BLACK OLIVES
○ OTHER		

CHEESE

○ GREASY	○ STINGY
○ SMOKEY	○ STINKY
○ CREAMY	○ SALTY

SAUCE

○ SWEET	○ SAVORY
○ TANGY	○ SPICY
○ THIN	○ CHUNKY

FRESHNESS

○1 ○2 ○3 ○4 ○5

CHEESE TO SAUCE RATIO (CSR)

CHEESE	☐☐☐☐☐☐☐
SAUCE	☐☐☐☐☐☐☐

CRUST SIZE	CRUST	
○ THIN	○ BUTTERY	○ CRISPY
○ MEDIUM	○ SPONGY	○ BUBBLY
○ LARGE	○ CHEWY	○ OTHER

CRUST

○1 ○2 ○3 ○4 ○5

STYLE ○ NY ○ CHICAGO ○ OTHER

COMMENTS

MY RATING	○1 ○2 ○3 ○4 ○5 ○6 ○7 ○8 ○9 ○10	EAT AGAIN?	○ YES ○ NO

Pizza Log

DATE	
PIZZERIA	
NEIGHBORHOOD	

TOPPINGS		
○ CHEESE	○ MUSHROOMS	○ ONIONS
○ PINEAPPLE	○ BACON	○ TUNA
○ GREEN PEPPER	○ SAUSAGE	○ BLACK OLIVES
○ OTHER		

CHEESE	
○ GREASY	○ STINGY
○ SMOKEY	○ STINKY
○ CREAMY	○ SALTY

SAUCE	
○ SWEET	○ SAVORY
○ TANGY	○ SPICY
○ THIN	○ CHUNKY

CHEESE TO SAUCE RATIO (CSR)	
CHEESE	☐ ☐ ☐ ☐ ☐ ☐ ☐
SAUCE	☐ ☐ ☐ ☐ ☐ ☐ ☐

FRESHNESS

○1 ○2 ○3 ○4 ○5

CRUST SIZE	CRUST	
○ THIN	○ BUTTERY	○ CRISPY
○ MEDIUM	○ SPONGY	○ BUBBLY
○ LARGE	○ CHEWY	○ OTHER

CRUST

○1 ○2 ○3 ○4 ○5

STYLE	○ NY ○ CHICAGO ○ OTHER

COMMENTS

MY RATING	○1 ○2 ○3 ○4 ○5 ○6 ○7 ○8 ○9 ○10	EAT AGAIN?	○ YES ○ NO

Pizza Log

DATE	
PIZZERIA	
NEIGHBORHOOD	

TOPPINGS		
O CHEESE	O MUSHROOMS	O ONIONS
O PINEAPPLE	O BACON	O TUNA
O GREEN PEPPER	O SAUSAGE	O BLACK OLIVES
O OTHER		

CHEESE	
O GREASY	O STINGY
O SMOKEY	O STINKY
O CREAMY	O SALTY

SAUCE	
O SWEET	O SAVORY
O TANGY	O SPICY
O THIN	O CHUNKY

FRESHNESS

O 1 O 2 O 3 O 4 O 5

CHEESE TO SAUCE RATIO (CSR)	
CHEESE	☐☐☐☐☐☐☐
SAUCE	☐☐☐☐☐☐☐

CRUST SIZE	CRUST	
O THIN	O BUTTERY	O CRISPY
O MEDIUM	O SPONGY	O BUBBLY
O LARGE	O CHEWY	O OTHER

CRUST

O 1 O 2 O 3 O 4 O 5

STYLE O NY O CHICAGO O OTHER

COMMENTS

MY RATING O 1 O 2 O 3 O 4 O 5 O 6 O 7 O 8 O 9 O 10

EAT AGAIN? O YES O NO

Pizza Log

DATE	
PIZZERIA	
NEIGHBORHOOD	

TOPPINGS		
○ CHEESE	○ MUSHROOMS	○ ONIONS
○ PINEAPPLE	○ BACON	○ TUNA
○ GREEN PEPPER	○ SAUSAGE	○ BLACK OLIVES
○ OTHER		

CHEESE	
○ GREASY	○ STINGY
○ SMOKEY	○ STINKY
○ CREAMY	○ SALTY

SAUCE	
○ SWEET	○ SAVORY
○ TANGY	○ SPICY
○ THIN	○ CHUNKY

CHEESE TO SAUCE RATIO (CSR)	
CHEESE	☐☐☐☐☐☐☐
SAUCE	☐☐☐☐☐☐☐

FRESHNESS

○ 1 ○ 2 ○ 3 ○ 4 ○ 5

CRUST SIZE
○ THIN
○ MEDIUM
○ LARGE

CRUST	
○ BUTTERY	○ CRISPY
○ SPONGY	○ BUBBLY
○ CHEWY	○ OTHER

CRUST

○ 1 ○ 2 ○ 3 ○ 4 ○ 5

STYLE ○ NY ○ CHICAGO ○ OTHER

COMMENTS

MY RATING ○ 1 ○ 2 ○ 3 ○ 4 ○ 5 ○ 6 ○ 7 ○ 8 ○ 9 ○ 10

EAT AGAIN? ○ YES ○ NO

Pizza Log

DATE	
PIZZERIA	
NEIGHBORHOOD	

TOPPINGS

- ○ CHEESE ○ MUSHROOMS ○ ONIONS
- ○ PINEAPPLE ○ BACON ○ TUNA
- ○ GREEN PEPPER ○ SAUSAGE ○ BLACK OLIVES
- ○ OTHER

CHEESE

- ○ GREASY ○ STINGY
- ○ SMOKEY ○ STINKY
- ○ CREAMY ○ SALTY

SAUCE

- ○ SWEET ○ SAVORY
- ○ TANGY ○ SPICY
- ○ THIN ○ CHUNKY

CHEESE TO SAUCE RATIO (CSR)

CHEESE	□□□□□□□
SAUCE	□□□□□□□

FRESHNESS

○ 1 ○ 2 ○ 3 ○ 4 ○ 5

CRUST SIZE

- ○ THIN
- ○ MEDIUM
- ○ LARGE

CRUST

- ○ BUTTERY ○ CRISPY
- ○ SPONGY ○ BUBBLY
- ○ CHEWY ○ OTHER

CRUST

○ 1 ○ 2 ○ 3 ○ 4 ○ 5

STYLE ○ NY ○ CHICAGO ○ OTHER

COMMENTS

MY RATING ○1 ○2 ○3 ○4 ○5 ○6 ○7 ○8 ○9 ○10

EAT AGAIN? ○ YES ○ NO

Pizza Log

DATE	
PIZZERIA	
NEIGHBORHOOD	

TOPPINGS		
○ CHEESE	○ MUSHROOMS	○ ONIONS
○ PINEAPPLE	○ BACON	○ TUNA
○ GREEN PEPPER	○ SAUSAGE	○ BLACK OLIVES
○ OTHER		

CHEESE	
○ GREASY	○ STINGY
○ SMOKEY	○ STINKY
○ CREAMY	○ SALTY

SAUCE	
○ SWEET	○ SAVORY
○ TANGY	○ SPICY
○ THIN	○ CHUNKY

CHEESE TO SAUCE RATIO (CSR)	
CHEESE	☐ ☐ ☐ ☐ ☐ ☐ ☐
SAUCE	☐ ☐ ☐ ☐ ☐ ☐ ☐

FRESHNESS

○ 1 ○ 2 ○ 3 ○ 4 ○ 5

CRUST SIZE	CRUST	
○ THIN	○ BUTTERY	○ CRISPY
○ MEDIUM	○ SPONGY	○ BUBBLY
○ LARGE	○ CHEWY	○ OTHER

CRUST

○ 1 ○ 2 ○ 3 ○ 4 ○ 5

STYLE	○ NY ○ CHICAGO ○ OTHER

COMMENTS

MY RATING	○1 ○2 ○3 ○4 ○5 ○6 ○7 ○8 ○9 ○10	EAT AGAIN?	○ YES ○ NO

Pizza Log

DATE	
PIZZERIA	
NEIGHBORHOOD	

TOPPINGS

O CHEESE	O MUSHROOMS	O ONIONS
O PINEAPPLE	O BACON	O TUNA
O GREEN PEPPER	O SAUSAGE	O BLACK OLIVES

O OTHER

CHEESE

O GREASY	O STINGY
O SMOKEY	O STINKY
O CREAMY	O SALTY

SAUCE

O SWEET	O SAVORY
O TANGY	O SPICY
O THIN	O CHUNKY

FRESHNESS

O 1 O 2 O 3 O 4 O 5

CHEESE TO SAUCE RATIO (CSR)

CHEESE	☐☐☐☐☐☐☐
SAUCE	☐☐☐☐☐☐☐

CRUST SIZE

O THIN
O MEDIUM
O LARGE

CRUST

O BUTTERY	O CRISPY
O SPONGY	O BUBBLY
O CHEWY	O OTHER

CRUST

O 1 O 2 O 3 O 4 O 5

STYLE O NY O CHICAGO O OTHER

COMMENTS

MY RATING O1 O2 O3 O4 O5 O6 O7 O8 O9 O10

EAT AGAIN? O YES O NO

Pizza Log

DATE	
PIZZERIA	
NEIGHBORHOOD	

TOPPINGS

○ CHEESE	○ MUSHROOMS	○ ONIONS
○ PINEAPPLE	○ BACON	○ TUNA
○ GREEN PEPPER	○ SAUSAGE	○ BLACK OLIVES
○ OTHER		

CHEESE

○ GREASY	○ STINGY
○ SMOKEY	○ STINKY
○ CREAMY	○ SALTY

SAUCE

○ SWEET	○ SAVORY
○ TANGY	○ SPICY
○ THIN	○ CHUNKY

CHEESE TO SAUCE RATIO (CSR)

CHEESE	☐ ☐ ☐ ☐ ☐ ☐ ☐
SAUCE	☐ ☐ ☐ ☐ ☐ ☐ ☐

FRESHNESS

○ 1 ○ 2 ○ 3 ○ 4 ○ 5

CRUST SIZE

○ THIN
○ MEDIUM
○ LARGE

CRUST

○ BUTTERY	○ CRISPY
○ SPONGY	○ BUBBLY
○ CHEWY	○ OTHER

CRUST

○ 1 ○ 2 ○ 3 ○ 4 ○ 5

STYLE ○ NY ○ CHICAGO ○ OTHER

COMMENTS

MY RATING	○1 ○2 ○3 ○4 ○5 ○6 ○7 ○8 ○9 ○10	EAT AGAIN?	○ YES ○ NO

Pizza Log

DATE	
PIZZERIA	
NEIGHBORHOOD	

TOPPINGS		
○ CHEESE	○ MUSHROOMS	○ ONIONS
○ PINEAPPLE	○ BACON	○ TUNA
○ GREEN PEPPER	○ SAUSAGE	○ BLACK OLIVES
○ OTHER		

CHEESE	
○ GREASY	○ STINGY
○ SMOKEY	○ STINKY
○ CREAMY	○ SALTY

SAUCE	
○ SWEET	○ SAVORY
○ TANGY	○ SPICY
○ THIN	○ CHUNKY

FRESHNESS

○ 1 ○ 2 ○ 3 ○ 4 ○ 5

CHEESE TO SAUCE RATIO (CSR)	
CHEESE	☐☐☐☐☐☐☐
SAUCE	☐☐☐☐☐☐☐

CRUST SIZE	CRUST	
○ THIN	○ BUTTERY	○ CRISPY
○ MEDIUM	○ SPONGY	○ BUBBLY
○ LARGE	○ CHEWY	○ OTHER

CRUST

○ 1 ○ 2 ○ 3 ○ 4 ○ 5

STYLE	○ NY ○ CHICAGO ○ OTHER

COMMENTS

MY RATING	○ 1 ○ 2 ○ 3 ○ 4 ○ 5 ○ 6 ○ 7 ○ 8 ○ 9 ○ 10	EAT AGAIN?	○ YES ○ NO

Pizza Log

DATE	
PIZZERIA	
NEIGHBORHOOD	

TOPPINGS		
○ CHEESE	○ MUSHROOMS	○ ONIONS
○ PINEAPPLE	○ BACON	○ TUNA
○ GREEN PEPPER	○ SAUSAGE	○ BLACK OLIVES
○ OTHER		

CHEESE	
○ GREASY	○ STINGY
○ SMOKEY	○ STINKY
○ CREAMY	○ SALTY

SAUCE	
○ SWEET	○ SAVORY
○ TANGY	○ SPICY
○ THIN	○ CHUNKY

CHEESE TO SAUCE RATIO (CSR)	
CHEESE	☐☐☐☐☐☐☐
SAUCE	☐☐☐☐☐☐☐

FRESHNESS

○1 ○2 ○3 ○4 ○5

CRUST SIZE	CRUST	
○ THIN	○ BUTTERY	○ CRISPY
○ MEDIUM	○ SPONGY	○ BUBBLY
○ LARGE	○ CHEWY	○ OTHER

CRUST

○1 ○2 ○3 ○4 ○5

STYLE	○ NY ○ CHICAGO ○ OTHER

COMMENTS

MY RATING	○1 ○2 ○3 ○4 ○5 ○6 ○7 ○8 ○9 ○10	EAT AGAIN?	○ YES ○ NO

Pizza Log

DATE	
PIZZERIA	
NEIGHBORHOOD	

TOPPINGS

○ CHEESE	○ MUSHROOMS	○ ONIONS
○ PINEAPPLE	○ BACON	○ TUNA
○ GREEN PEPPER	○ SAUSAGE	○ BLACK OLIVES
○ OTHER		

CHEESE

○ GREASY	○ STINGY
○ SMOKEY	○ STINKY
○ CREAMY	○ SALTY

SAUCE

○ SWEET	○ SAVORY
○ TANGY	○ SPICY
○ THIN	○ CHUNKY

CHEESE TO SAUCE RATIO (CSR)

CHEESE	□ □ □ □ □ □ □
SAUCE	□ □ □ □ □ □ □

FRESHNESS

○1 ○2 ○3 ○4 ○5

CRUST SIZE

○ THIN
○ MEDIUM
○ LARGE

CRUST

○ BUTTERY	○ CRISPY
○ SPONGY	○ BUBBLY
○ CHEWY	○ OTHER

CRUST

○1 ○2 ○3 ○4 ○5

STYLE ○ NY ○ CHICAGO ○ OTHER

COMMENTS

MY RATING ○1 ○2 ○3 ○4 ○5 ○6 ○7 ○8 ○9 ○10

EAT AGAIN? ○ YES ○ NO

Pizza Log

DATE	
PIZZERIA	
NEIGHBORHOOD	

TOPPINGS		
○ CHEESE	○ MUSHROOMS	○ ONIONS
○ PINEAPPLE	○ BACON	○ TUNA
○ GREEN PEPPER	○ SAUSAGE	○ BLACK OLIVES
○ OTHER		

CHEESE	
○ GREASY	○ STINGY
○ SMOKEY	○ STINKY
○ CREAMY	○ SALTY

SAUCE	
○ SWEET	○ SAVORY
○ TANGY	○ SPICY
○ THIN	○ CHUNKY

CHEESE TO SAUCE RATIO (CSR)	
CHEESE	☐☐☐☐☐☐☐
SAUCE	☐☐☐☐☐☐☐

FRESHNESS

○ 1 ○ 2 ○ 3 ○ 4 ○ 5

CRUST SIZE	CRUST	
○ THIN	○ BUTTERY	○ CRISPY
○ MEDIUM	○ SPONGY	○ BUBBLY
○ LARGE	○ CHEWY	○ OTHER

CRUST

○ 1 ○ 2 ○ 3 ○ 4 ○ 5

STYLE	○ NY ○ CHICAGO ○ OTHER

COMMENTS

MY RATING	○1 ○2 ○3 ○4 ○5 ○6 ○7 ○8 ○9 ○10	EAT AGAIN?	○ YES ○ NO

Pizza Log

DATE	
PIZZERIA	
NEIGHBORHOOD	

TOPPINGS		
○ CHEESE	○ MUSHROOMS	○ ONIONS
○ PINEAPPLE	○ BACON	○ TUNA
○ GREEN PEPPER	○ SAUSAGE	○ BLACK OLIVES
○ OTHER		

CHEESE	
○ GREASY	○ STINGY
○ SMOKEY	○ STINKY
○ CREAMY	○ SALTY

SAUCE	
○ SWEET	○ SAVORY
○ TANGY	○ SPICY
○ THIN	○ CHUNKY

CHEESE TO SAUCE RATIO (CSR)	
CHEESE	□□□□□□□
SAUCE	□□□□□□□

FRESHNESS

○1 ○2 ○3 ○4 ○5

CRUST SIZE	CRUST	
○ THIN	○ BUTTERY	○ CRISPY
○ MEDIUM	○ SPONGY	○ BUBBLY
○ LARGE	○ CHEWY	○ OTHER

CRUST

○1 ○2 ○3 ○4 ○5

STYLE	○ NY ○ CHICAGO ○ OTHER

COMMENTS

MY RATING	○1 ○2 ○3 ○4 ○5 ○6 ○7 ○8 ○9 ○10	EAT AGAIN?	○ YES ○ NO

Pizza Log

DATE	
PIZZERIA	
NEIGHBORHOOD	

TOPPINGS		
○ CHEESE	○ MUSHROOMS	○ ONIONS
○ PINEAPPLE	○ BACON	○ TUNA
○ GREEN PEPPER	○ SAUSAGE	○ BLACK OLIVES
○ OTHER		

CHEESE	
○ GREASY	○ STINGY
○ SMOKEY	○ STINKY
○ CREAMY	○ SALTY

SAUCE	
○ SWEET	○ SAVORY
○ TANGY	○ SPICY
○ THIN	○ CHUNKY

CHEESE TO SAUCE RATIO (CSR)	
CHEESE	□□□□□□□
SAUCE	□□□□□□□

FRESHNESS

○1 ○2 ○3 ○4 ○5

CRUST SIZE	CRUST	
○ THIN	○ BUTTERY	○ CRISPY
○ MEDIUM	○ SPONGY	○ BUBBLY
○ LARGE	○ CHEWY	○ OTHER

CRUST

○1 ○2 ○3 ○4 ○5

STYLE	○ NY ○ CHICAGO ○ OTHER

COMMENTS

MY RATING	○1 ○2 ○3 ○4 ○5 ○6 ○7 ○8 ○9 ○10	EAT AGAIN?	○ YES ○ NO

Pizza Log

DATE	
PIZZERIA	
NEIGHBORHOOD	

TOPPINGS

O CHEESE	O MUSHROOMS	O ONIONS
O PINEAPPLE	O BACON	O TUNA
O GREEN PEPPER	O SAUSAGE	O BLACK OLIVES
O OTHER		

CHEESE

O GREASY	O STINGY
O SMOKEY	O STINKY
O CREAMY	O SALTY

SAUCE

O SWEET	O SAVORY
O TANGY	O SPICY
O THIN	O CHUNKY

CHEESE TO SAUCE RATIO (CSR)

CHEESE	☐☐☐☐☐☐☐
SAUCE	☐☐☐☐☐☐☐

FRESHNESS

O 1 O 2 O 3 O 4 O 5

CRUST SIZE	CRUST	
O THIN	O BUTTERY	O CRISPY
O MEDIUM	O SPONGY	O BUBBLY
O LARGE	O CHEWY	O OTHER

CRUST

O 1 O 2 O 3 O 4 O 5

STYLE	O NY O CHICAGO O OTHER

COMMENTS

MY RATING	O1 O2 O3 O4 O5 O6 O7 O8 O9 O10	EAT AGAIN?	O YES O NO

Pizza Log

DATE	
PIZZERIA	
NEIGHBORHOOD	

TOPPINGS

○ CHEESE	○ MUSHROOMS	○ ONIONS
○ PINEAPPLE	○ BACON	○ TUNA
○ GREEN PEPPER	○ SAUSAGE	○ BLACK OLIVES
○ OTHER		

CHEESE

○ GREASY	○ STINGY
○ SMOKEY	○ STINKY
○ CREAMY	○ SALTY

SAUCE

○ SWEET	○ SAVORY
○ TANGY	○ SPICY
○ THIN	○ CHUNKY

CHEESE TO SAUCE RATIO (CSR)

CHEESE	☐☐☐☐☐☐☐
SAUCE	☐☐☐☐☐☐☐

FRESHNESS

○1 ○2 ○3 ○4 ○5

CRUST SIZE

○ THIN
○ MEDIUM
○ LARGE

CRUST

○ BUTTERY	○ CRISPY
○ SPONGY	○ BUBBLY
○ CHEWY	○ OTHER

CRUST

○1 ○2 ○3 ○4 ○5

STYLE	○ NY ○ CHICAGO ○ OTHER

COMMENTS

MY RATING	○1 ○2 ○3 ○4 ○5 ○6 ○7 ○8 ○9 ○10	EAT AGAIN?	○ YES ○ NO

Pizza Log

DATE	
PIZZERIA	
NEIGHBORHOOD	

TOPPINGS

○ CHEESE	○ MUSHROOMS	○ ONIONS
○ PINEAPPLE	○ BACON	○ TUNA
○ GREEN PEPPER	○ SAUSAGE	○ BLACK OLIVES
○ OTHER		

CHEESE

○ GREASY	○ STINGY
○ SMOKEY	○ STINKY
○ CREAMY	○ SALTY

SAUCE

○ SWEET	○ SAVORY
○ TANGY	○ SPICY
○ THIN	○ CHUNKY

CHEESE TO SAUCE RATIO (CSR)

CHEESE	☐☐☐☐☐☐☐
SAUCE	☐☐☐☐☐☐☐

FRESHNESS

○1 ○2 ○3 ○4 ○5

CRUST SIZE

○ THIN
○ MEDIUM
○ LARGE

CRUST

○ BUTTERY	○ CRISPY
○ SPONGY	○ BUBBLY
○ CHEWY	○ OTHER

CRUST

○1 ○2 ○3 ○4 ○5

STYLE ○ NY ○ CHICAGO ○ OTHER

COMMENTS

MY RATING ○1 ○2 ○3 ○4 ○5 ○6 ○7 ○8 ○9 ○10

EAT AGAIN? ○ YES ○ NO

Pizza Log

DATE	
PIZZERIA	
NEIGHBORHOOD	

TOPPINGS		
○ CHEESE	○ MUSHROOMS	○ ONIONS
○ PINEAPPLE	○ BACON	○ TUNA
○ GREEN PEPPER	○ SAUSAGE	○ BLACK OLIVES
○ OTHER		

CHEESE	
○ GREASY	○ STINGY
○ SMOKEY	○ STINKY
○ CREAMY	○ SALTY

SAUCE	
○ SWEET	○ SAVORY
○ TANGY	○ SPICY
○ THIN	○ CHUNKY

CHEESE TO SAUCE RATIO (CSR)	
CHEESE	□ □ □ □ □ □ □
SAUCE	□ □ □ □ □ □ □

FRESHNESS

○ 1 ○ 2 ○ 3 ○ 4 ○ 5

CRUST SIZE	CRUST	
○ THIN	○ BUTTERY	○ CRISPY
○ MEDIUM	○ SPONGY	○ BUBBLY
○ LARGE	○ CHEWY	○ OTHER

CRUST

○ 1 ○ 2 ○ 3 ○ 4 ○ 5

STYLE	○ NY ○ CHICAGO ○ OTHER

COMMENTS

MY RATING	○1 ○2 ○3 ○4 ○5 ○6 ○7 ○8 ○9 ○10	EAT AGAIN?	○ YES ○ NO

Pizza Log

DATE	
PIZZERIA	
NEIGHBORHOOD	

TOPPINGS

○ CHEESE	○ MUSHROOMS	○ ONIONS
○ PINEAPPLE	○ BACON	○ TUNA
○ GREEN PEPPER	○ SAUSAGE	○ BLACK OLIVES
○ OTHER		

CHEESE

○ GREASY	○ STINGY
○ SMOKEY	○ STINKY
○ CREAMY	○ SALTY

SAUCE

○ SWEET	○ SAVORY
○ TANGY	○ SPICY
○ THIN	○ CHUNKY

CHEESE TO SAUCE RATIO (CSR)

CHEESE	☐☐☐☐☐☐☐
SAUCE	☐☐☐☐☐☐☐

FRESHNESS

○1 ○2 ○3 ○4 ○5

CRUST SIZE

○ THIN
○ MEDIUM
○ LARGE

CRUST

○ BUTTERY	○ CRISPY
○ SPONGY	○ BUBBLY
○ CHEWY	○ OTHER

CRUST

○1 ○2 ○3 ○4 ○5

STYLE ○ NY ○ CHICAGO ○ OTHER

COMMENTS

MY RATING ○1 ○2 ○3 ○4 ○5 ○6 ○7 ○8 ○9 ○10

EAT AGAIN? ○ YES ○ NO

Pizza Log

DATE	
PIZZERIA	
NEIGHBORHOOD	

TOPPINGS

○ CHEESE	○ MUSHROOMS	○ ONIONS
○ PINEAPPLE	○ BACON	○ TUNA
○ GREEN PEPPER	○ SAUSAGE	○ BLACK OLIVES
○ OTHER		

CHEESE

○ GREASY	○ STINGY
○ SMOKEY	○ STINKY
○ CREAMY	○ SALTY

SAUCE

○ SWEET	○ SAVORY
○ TANGY	○ SPICY
○ THIN	○ CHUNKY

CHEESE TO SAUCE RATIO (CSR)

CHEESE	□□□□□□□
SAUCE	□□□□□□□

FRESHNESS

○ 1 ○ 2 ○ 3 ○ 4 ○ 5

CRUST SIZE

○ THIN
○ MEDIUM
○ LARGE

CRUST

○ BUTTERY	○ CRISPY
○ SPONGY	○ BUBBLY
○ CHEWY	○ OTHER

CRUST

○ 1 ○ 2 ○ 3 ○ 4 ○ 5

STYLE	○ NY ○ CHICAGO ○ OTHER

COMMENTS

MY RATING	○1 ○2 ○3 ○4 ○5 ○6 ○7 ○8 ○9 ○10	EAT AGAIN?	○ YES ○ NO

Pizza Log

DATE	
PIZZERIA	
NEIGHBORHOOD	

TOPPINGS

○ CHEESE	○ MUSHROOMS	○ ONIONS
○ PINEAPPLE	○ BACON	○ TUNA
○ GREEN PEPPER	○ SAUSAGE	○ BLACK OLIVES
○ OTHER		

CHEESE

○ GREASY	○ STINGY
○ SMOKEY	○ STINKY
○ CREAMY	○ SALTY

SAUCE

○ SWEET	○ SAVORY
○ TANGY	○ SPICY
○ THIN	○ CHUNKY

CHEESE TO SAUCE RATIO (CSR)

CHEESE	□□□□□□□
SAUCE	□□□□□□□

FRESHNESS

○1 ○2 ○3 ○4 ○5

CRUST SIZE

○ THIN
○ MEDIUM
○ LARGE

CRUST

○ BUTTERY	○ CRISPY
○ SPONGY	○ BUBBLY
○ CHEWY	○ OTHER

CRUST

○1 ○2 ○3 ○4 ○5

STYLE	○ NY ○ CHICAGO ○ OTHER

COMMENTS

MY RATING	○1 ○2 ○3 ○4 ○5 ○6 ○7 ○8 ○9 ○10	EAT AGAIN?	○ YES ○ NO

Pizza Log

DATE	
PIZZERIA	
NEIGHBORHOOD	

TOPPINGS		
○ CHEESE	○ MUSHROOMS	○ ONIONS
○ PINEAPPLE	○ BACON	○ TUNA
○ GREEN PEPPER	○ SAUSAGE	○ BLACK OLIVES
○ OTHER		

CHEESE	
○ GREASY	○ STINGY
○ SMOKEY	○ STINKY
○ CREAMY	○ SALTY

SAUCE	
○ SWEET	○ SAVORY
○ TANGY	○ SPICY
○ THIN	○ CHUNKY

CHEESE TO SAUCE RATIO (CSR)	
CHEESE	☐ ☐ ☐ ☐ ☐ ☐ ☐
SAUCE	☐ ☐ ☐ ☐ ☐ ☐ ☐

FRESHNESS

○ 1 ○ 2 ○ 3 ○ 4 ○ 5

CRUST SIZE	CRUST	
○ THIN	○ BUTTERY	○ CRISPY
○ MEDIUM	○ SPONGY	○ BUBBLY
○ LARGE	○ CHEWY	○ OTHER

CRUST

○ 1 ○ 2 ○ 3 ○ 4 ○ 5

STYLE	○ NY ○ CHICAGO ○ OTHER

COMMENTS

MY RATING	○ 1 ○ 2 ○ 3 ○ 4 ○ 5 ○ 6 ○ 7 ○ 8 ○ 9 ○ 10	EAT AGAIN?	○ YES ○ NO

Pizza Log

DATE	
PIZZERIA	
NEIGHBORHOOD	

TOPPINGS		
○ CHEESE	○ MUSHROOMS	○ ONIONS
○ PINEAPPLE	○ BACON	○ TUNA
○ GREEN PEPPER	○ SAUSAGE	○ BLACK OLIVES
○ OTHER		

CHEESE	
○ GREASY	○ STINGY
○ SMOKEY	○ STINKY
○ CREAMY	○ SALTY

SAUCE	
○ SWEET	○ SAVORY
○ TANGY	○ SPICY
○ THIN	○ CHUNKY

CHEESE TO SAUCE RATIO (CSR)	
CHEESE	□ □ □ □ □ □ □
SAUCE	□ □ □ □ □ □ □

FRESHNESS

○1 ○2 ○3 ○4 ○5

CRUST SIZE	CRUST	
○ THIN	○ BUTTERY	○ CRISPY
○ MEDIUM	○ SPONGY	○ BUBBLY
○ LARGE	○ CHEWY	○ OTHER

CRUST

○1 ○2 ○3 ○4 ○5

STYLE	○ NY ○ CHICAGO ○ OTHER

COMMENTS

MY RATING	○1 ○2 ○3 ○4 ○5 ○6 ○7 ○8 ○9 ○10	EAT AGAIN?	○ YES ○ NO

Pizza Log

DATE	
PIZZERIA	
NEIGHBORHOOD	

TOPPINGS

○ CHEESE	○ MUSHROOMS	○ ONIONS
○ PINEAPPLE	○ BACON	○ TUNA
○ GREEN PEPPER	○ SAUSAGE	○ BLACK OLIVES
○ OTHER		

CHEESE

○ GREASY	○ STINGY
○ SMOKEY	○ STINKY
○ CREAMY	○ SALTY

SAUCE

○ SWEET	○ SAVORY
○ TANGY	○ SPICY
○ THIN	○ CHUNKY

CHEESE TO SAUCE RATIO (CSR)

CHEESE	□□□□□□□
SAUCE	□□□□□□□

FRESHNESS

○1 ○2 ○3 ○4 ○5

CRUST SIZE

○ THIN
○ MEDIUM
○ LARGE

CRUST

○ BUTTERY	○ CRISPY
○ SPONGY	○ BUBBLY
○ CHEWY	○ OTHER

CRUST

○1 ○2 ○3 ○4 ○5

STYLE ○ NY ○ CHICAGO ○ OTHER

COMMENTS

MY RATING	○1 ○2 ○3 ○4 ○5 ○6 ○7 ○8 ○9 ○10	EAT AGAIN?	○ YES ○ NO

Pizza Log

DATE	
PIZZERIA	
NEIGHBORHOOD	

TOPPINGS

○ CHEESE	○ MUSHROOMS	○ ONIONS
○ PINEAPPLE	○ BACON	○ TUNA
○ GREEN PEPPER	○ SAUSAGE	○ BLACK OLIVES
○ OTHER		

CHEESE

○ GREASY	○ STINGY
○ SMOKEY	○ STINKY
○ CREAMY	○ SALTY

SAUCE

○ SWEET	○ SAVORY
○ TANGY	○ SPICY
○ THIN	○ CHUNKY

FRESHNESS

○1 ○2 ○3 ○4 ○5

CHEESE TO SAUCE RATIO (CSR)

CHEESE	□□□□□□□
SAUCE	□□□□□□□

CRUST SIZE

○ THIN
○ MEDIUM
○ LARGE

CRUST

○ BUTTERY	○ CRISPY
○ SPONGY	○ BUBBLY
○ CHEWY	○ OTHER

CRUST

○1 ○2 ○3 ○4 ○5

STYLE ○ NY ○ CHICAGO ○ OTHER

COMMENTS

MY RATING ○1 ○2 ○3 ○4 ○5 ○6 ○7 ○8 ○9 ○10

EAT AGAIN? ○ YES ○ NO

Pizza Log

DATE	
PIZZERIA	
NEIGHBORHOOD	

TOPPINGS		
○ CHEESE	○ MUSHROOMS	○ ONIONS
○ PINEAPPLE	○ BACON	○ TUNA
○ GREEN PEPPER	○ SAUSAGE	○ BLACK OLIVES
○ OTHER		

CHEESE	
○ GREASY	○ STINGY
○ SMOKEY	○ STINKY
○ CREAMY	○ SALTY

SAUCE	
○ SWEET	○ SAVORY
○ TANGY	○ SPICY
○ THIN	○ CHUNKY

CHEESE TO SAUCE RATIO (CSR)	
CHEESE	☐ ☐ ☐ ☐ ☐ ☐ ☐
SAUCE	☐ ☐ ☐ ☐ ☐ ☐ ☐

FRESHNESS

○ 1 ○ 2 ○ 3 ○ 4 ○ 5

CRUST SIZE	CRUST	
○ THIN	○ BUTTERY	○ CRISPY
○ MEDIUM	○ SPONGY	○ BUBBLY
○ LARGE	○ CHEWY	○ OTHER

CRUST

○ 1 ○ 2 ○ 3 ○ 4 ○ 5

STYLE	○ NY ○ CHICAGO ○ OTHER

COMMENTS

MY RATING	○1 ○2 ○3 ○4 ○5 ○6 ○7 ○8 ○9 ○10	EAT AGAIN?	○ YES ○ NO

Pizza Log

DATE	
PIZZERIA	
NEIGHBORHOOD	

TOPPINGS

○ CHEESE	○ MUSHROOMS	○ ONIONS
○ PINEAPPLE	○ BACON	○ TUNA
○ GREEN PEPPER	○ SAUSAGE	○ BLACK OLIVES
○ OTHER		

CHEESE

○ GREASY	○ STINGY
○ SMOKEY	○ STINKY
○ CREAMY	○ SALTY

SAUCE

○ SWEET	○ SAVORY
○ TANGY	○ SPICY
○ THIN	○ CHUNKY

CHEESE TO SAUCE RATIO (CSR)

CHEESE	☐☐☐☐☐☐☐
SAUCE	☐☐☐☐☐☐☐

FRESHNESS

○1 ○2 ○3 ○4 ○5

CRUST SIZE

○ THIN
○ MEDIUM
○ LARGE

CRUST

○ BUTTERY	○ CRISPY
○ SPONGY	○ BUBBLY
○ CHEWY	○ OTHER

CRUST

○1 ○2 ○3 ○4 ○5

STYLE ○ NY ○ CHICAGO ○ OTHER

COMMENTS

MY RATING ○1 ○2 ○3 ○4 ○5 ○6 ○7 ○8 ○9 ○10

EAT AGAIN? ○ YES ○ NO

Pizza Log

DATE	
PIZZERIA	
NEIGHBORHOOD	

TOPPINGS

○ CHEESE	○ MUSHROOMS	○ ONIONS
○ PINEAPPLE	○ BACON	○ TUNA
○ GREEN PEPPER	○ SAUSAGE	○ BLACK OLIVES
○ OTHER		

CHEESE

○ GREASY	○ STINGY
○ SMOKEY	○ STINKY
○ CREAMY	○ SALTY

SAUCE

○ SWEET	○ SAVORY
○ TANGY	○ SPICY
○ THIN	○ CHUNKY

CHEESE TO SAUCE RATIO (CSR)

CHEESE	☐ ☐ ☐ ☐ ☐ ☐ ☐
SAUCE	☐ ☐ ☐ ☐ ☐ ☐ ☐

FRESHNESS

○ 1 ○ 2 ○ 3 ○ 4 ○ 5

CRUST SIZE

CRUST SIZE	**CRUST**	
○ THIN	○ BUTTERY	○ CRISPY
○ MEDIUM	○ SPONGY	○ BUBBLY
○ LARGE	○ CHEWY	○ OTHER

CRUST

○ 1 ○ 2 ○ 3 ○ 4 ○ 5

STYLE ○ NY ○ CHICAGO ○ OTHER

COMMENTS

MY RATING	○1 ○2 ○3 ○4 ○5 ○6 ○7 ○8 ○9 ○10	EAT AGAIN?	○ YES ○ NO

Pizza Log

DATE	
PIZZERIA	
NEIGHBORHOOD	

TOPPINGS

O CHEESE	O MUSHROOMS	O ONIONS
O PINEAPPLE	O BACON	O TUNA
O GREEN PEPPER	O SAUSAGE	O BLACK OLIVES
O OTHER		

CHEESE

O GREASY	O STINGY
O SMOKEY	O STINKY
O CREAMY	O SALTY

SAUCE

O SWEET	O SAVORY
O TANGY	O SPICY
O THIN	O CHUNKY

CHEESE TO SAUCE RATIO (CSR)

CHEESE	☐☐☐☐☐☐☐
SAUCE	☐☐☐☐☐☐☐

FRESHNESS

O 1 O 2 O 3 O 4 O 5

CRUST SIZE

O THIN
O MEDIUM
O LARGE

CRUST

O BUTTERY	O CRISPY
O SPONGY	O BUBBLY
O CHEWY	O OTHER

CRUST

O 1 O 2 O 3 O 4 O 5

STYLE O NY O CHICAGO O OTHER

COMMENTS

MY RATING O1 O2 O3 O4 O5 O6 O7 O8 O9 O10

EAT AGAIN? O YES O NO

Pizza Log

DATE	
PIZZERIA	
NEIGHBORHOOD	

TOPPINGS		
○ CHEESE	○ MUSHROOMS	○ ONIONS
○ PINEAPPLE	○ BACON	○ TUNA
○ GREEN PEPPER	○ SAUSAGE	○ BLACK OLIVES
○ OTHER		

CHEESE	
○ GREASY	○ STINGY
○ SMOKEY	○ STINKY
○ CREAMY	○ SALTY

SAUCE	
○ SWEET	○ SAVORY
○ TANGY	○ SPICY
○ THIN	○ CHUNKY

CHEESE TO SAUCE RATIO (CSR)	
CHEESE	□□□□□□□
SAUCE	□□□□□□□

FRESHNESS

○ 1 ○ 2 ○ 3 ○ 4 ○ 5

CRUST SIZE	CRUST	
○ THIN	○ BUTTERY	○ CRISPY
○ MEDIUM	○ SPONGY	○ BUBBLY
○ LARGE	○ CHEWY	○ OTHER

CRUST

○ 1 ○ 2 ○ 3 ○ 4 ○ 5

STYLE	○ NY ○ CHICAGO ○ OTHER

COMMENTS

MY RATING	○1 ○2 ○3 ○4 ○5 ○6 ○7 ○8 ○9 ○10	EAT AGAIN?	○ YES ○ NO

Pizza Log

DATE	
PIZZERIA	
NEIGHBORHOOD	

TOPPINGS		
O CHEESE	O MUSHROOMS	O ONIONS
O PINEAPPLE	O BACON	O TUNA
O GREEN PEPPER	O SAUSAGE	O BLACK OLIVES
O OTHER		

CHEESE	
O GREASY	O STINGY
O SMOKEY	O STINKY
O CREAMY	O SALTY

SAUCE	
O SWEET	O SAVORY
O TANGY	O SPICY
O THIN	O CHUNKY

CHEESE TO SAUCE RATIO (CSR)	
CHEESE	☐ ☐ ☐ ☐ ☐ ☐ ☐
SAUCE	☐ ☐ ☐ ☐ ☐ ☐ ☐

FRESHNESS

O 1 O 2 O 3 O 4 O 5

CRUST SIZE	CRUST	
O THIN	O BUTTERY	O CRISPY
O MEDIUM	O SPONGY	O BUBBLY
O LARGE	O CHEWY	O OTHER

CRUST

O 1 O 2 O 3 O 4 O 5

STYLE	O NY O CHICAGO O OTHER

COMMENTS

MY RATING	O1 O2 O3 O4 O5 O6 O7 O8 O9 O10	EAT AGAIN?	O YES O NO

Pizza Log

DATE	
PIZZERIA	
NEIGHBORHOOD	

TOPPINGS

○ CHEESE	○ MUSHROOMS	○ ONIONS
○ PINEAPPLE	○ BACON	○ TUNA
○ GREEN PEPPER	○ SAUSAGE	○ BLACK OLIVES
○ OTHER		

CHEESE

○ GREASY	○ STINGY
○ SMOKEY	○ STINKY
○ CREAMY	○ SALTY

SAUCE

○ SWEET	○ SAVORY
○ TANGY	○ SPICY
○ THIN	○ CHUNKY

CHEESE TO SAUCE RATIO (CSR)

CHEESE	□□□□□□□
SAUCE	□□□□□□□

FRESHNESS

○1 ○2 ○3 ○4 ○5

CRUST SIZE	CRUST	
○ THIN	○ BUTTERY	○ CRISPY
○ MEDIUM	○ SPONGY	○ BUBBLY
○ LARGE	○ CHEWY	○ OTHER

CRUST

○1 ○2 ○3 ○4 ○5

STYLE ○ NY ○ CHICAGO ○ OTHER

COMMENTS

MY RATING	○1 ○2 ○3 ○4 ○5 ○6 ○7 ○8 ○9 ○10	EAT AGAIN?	○ YES ○ NO

Pizza Log

DATE	
PIZZERIA	
NEIGHBORHOOD	

TOPPINGS

○ CHEESE	○ MUSHROOMS	○ ONIONS
○ PINEAPPLE	○ BACON	○ TUNA
○ GREEN PEPPER	○ SAUSAGE	○ BLACK OLIVES
○ OTHER		

CHEESE

○ GREASY	○ STINGY
○ SMOKEY	○ STINKY
○ CREAMY	○ SALTY

SAUCE

○ SWEET	○ SAVORY
○ TANGY	○ SPICY
○ THIN	○ CHUNKY

FRESHNESS

○1 ○2 ○3 ○4 ○5

CHEESE TO SAUCE RATIO (CSR)

CHEESE	☐☐☐☐☐☐☐
SAUCE	☐☐☐☐☐☐☐

CRUST SIZE

○ THIN
○ MEDIUM
○ LARGE

CRUST

○ BUTTERY	○ CRISPY
○ SPONGY	○ BUBBLY
○ CHEWY	○ OTHER

CRUST

○1 ○2 ○3 ○4 ○5

STYLE ○ NY ○ CHICAGO ○ OTHER

COMMENTS

MY RATING ○1 ○2 ○3 ○4 ○5 ○6 ○7 ○8 ○9 ○10

EAT AGAIN? ○ YES ○ NO

Pizza Log

DATE	
PIZZERIA	
NEIGHBORHOOD	

TOPPINGS

○ CHEESE	○ MUSHROOMS	○ ONIONS
○ PINEAPPLE	○ BACON	○ TUNA
○ GREEN PEPPER	○ SAUSAGE	○ BLACK OLIVES
○ OTHER		

CHEESE

○ GREASY	○ STINGY
○ SMOKEY	○ STINKY
○ CREAMY	○ SALTY

SAUCE

○ SWEET	○ SAVORY
○ TANGY	○ SPICY
○ THIN	○ CHUNKY

CHEESE TO SAUCE RATIO (CSR)

CHEESE	□ □ □ □ □ □ □
SAUCE	□ □ □ □ □ □ □

FRESHNESS

○ 1 ○ 2 ○ 3 ○ 4 ○ 5

CRUST SIZE

○ THIN
○ MEDIUM
○ LARGE

CRUST

○ BUTTERY	○ CRISPY
○ SPONGY	○ BUBBLY
○ CHEWY	○ OTHER

CRUST

○ 1 ○ 2 ○ 3 ○ 4 ○ 5

STYLE ○ NY ○ CHICAGO ○ OTHER

COMMENTS

MY RATING ○ 1 ○ 2 ○ 3 ○ 4 ○ 5 ○ 6 ○ 7 ○ 8 ○ 9 ○ 10

EAT AGAIN? ○ YES ○ NO

Pizza Log

DATE	
PIZZERIA	
NEIGHBORHOOD	

TOPPINGS		
○ CHEESE	○ MUSHROOMS	○ ONIONS
○ PINEAPPLE	○ BACON	○ TUNA
○ GREEN PEPPER	○ SAUSAGE	○ BLACK OLIVES
○ OTHER		

CHEESE	
○ GREASY	○ STINGY
○ SMOKEY	○ STINKY
○ CREAMY	○ SALTY

SAUCE	
○ SWEET	○ SAVORY
○ TANGY	○ SPICY
○ THIN	○ CHUNKY

CHEESE TO SAUCE RATIO (CSR)	
CHEESE	□□□□□□□
SAUCE	□□□□□□□

FRESHNESS

○1 ○2 ○3 ○4 ○5

CRUST SIZE	CRUST	
○ THIN	○ BUTTERY	○ CRISPY
○ MEDIUM	○ SPONGY	○ BUBBLY
○ LARGE	○ CHEWY	○ OTHER

CRUST

○1 ○2 ○3 ○4 ○5

STYLE	○ NY ○ CHICAGO ○ OTHER

COMMENTS

MY RATING	○1 ○2 ○3 ○4 ○5 ○6 ○7 ○8 ○9 ○10	EAT AGAIN?	○ YES ○ NO

Pizza Log

DATE	
PIZZERIA	
NEIGHBORHOOD	

TOPPINGS

○ CHEESE	○ MUSHROOMS	○ ONIONS
○ PINEAPPLE	○ BACON	○ TUNA
○ GREEN PEPPER	○ SAUSAGE	○ BLACK OLIVES

○ OTHER

CHEESE

○ GREASY	○ STINGY
○ SMOKEY	○ STINKY
○ CREAMY	○ SALTY

SAUCE

○ SWEET	○ SAVORY
○ TANGY	○ SPICY
○ THIN	○ CHUNKY

CHEESE TO SAUCE RATIO (CSR)

CHEESE	☐ ☐ ☐ ☐ ☐ ☐ ☐
SAUCE	☐ ☐ ☐ ☐ ☐ ☐ ☐

FRESHNESS

○ 1 ○ 2 ○ 3 ○ 4 ○ 5

CRUST SIZE	CRUST	
○ THIN	○ BUTTERY	○ CRISPY
○ MEDIUM	○ SPONGY	○ BUBBLY
○ LARGE	○ CHEWY	○ OTHER

CRUST

○ 1 ○ 2 ○ 3 ○ 4 ○ 5

STYLE ○ NY ○ CHICAGO ○ OTHER

COMMENTS

MY RATING	○ 1 ○ 2 ○ 3 ○ 4 ○ 5 ○ 6 ○ 7 ○ 8 ○ 9 ○ 10	EAT AGAIN?	○ YES ○ NO

Pizza Log

DATE	
PIZZERIA	
NEIGHBORHOOD	

TOPPINGS

○ CHEESE	○ MUSHROOMS	○ ONIONS
○ PINEAPPLE	○ BACON	○ TUNA
○ GREEN PEPPER	○ SAUSAGE	○ BLACK OLIVES

○ OTHER

CHEESE

○ GREASY	○ STINGY
○ SMOKEY	○ STINKY
○ CREAMY	○ SALTY

SAUCE

○ SWEET	○ SAVORY
○ TANGY	○ SPICY
○ THIN	○ CHUNKY

CHEESE TO SAUCE RATIO (CSR)

CHEESE	☐☐☐☐☐☐☐
SAUCE	☐☐☐☐☐☐☐

FRESHNESS

○1 ○2 ○3 ○4 ○5

CRUST SIZE	CRUST	
○ THIN	○ BUTTERY	○ CRISPY
○ MEDIUM	○ SPONGY	○ BUBBLY
○ LARGE	○ CHEWY	○ OTHER

CRUST

○1 ○2 ○3 ○4 ○5

STYLE ○ NY ○ CHICAGO ○ OTHER

COMMENTS

MY RATING	○1 ○2 ○3 ○4 ○5 ○6 ○7 ○8 ○9 ○10	EAT AGAIN?	○ YES ○ NO

Pizza Log

DATE	
PIZZERIA	
NEIGHBORHOOD	

TOPPINGS

○ CHEESE	○ MUSHROOMS	○ ONIONS
○ PINEAPPLE	○ BACON	○ TUNA
○ GREEN PEPPER	○ SAUSAGE	○ BLACK OLIVES
○ OTHER		

CHEESE

○ GREASY	○ STINGY
○ SMOKEY	○ STINKY
○ CREAMY	○ SALTY

SAUCE

○ SWEET	○ SAVORY
○ TANGY	○ SPICY
○ THIN	○ CHUNKY

CHEESE TO SAUCE RATIO (CSR)

CHEESE	□ □ □ □ □ □ □
SAUCE	□ □ □ □ □ □ □

FRESHNESS

○1 ○2 ○3 ○4 ○5

CRUST SIZE	CRUST	
○ THIN	○ BUTTERY	○ CRISPY
○ MEDIUM	○ SPONGY	○ BUBBLY
○ LARGE	○ CHEWY	○ OTHER

CRUST

○1 ○2 ○3 ○4 ○5

STYLE	○ NY ○ CHICAGO ○ OTHER

COMMENTS

MY RATING	○1 ○2 ○3 ○4 ○5 ○6 ○7 ○8 ○9 ○10	EAT AGAIN?	○ YES ○ NO

Pizza Log

DATE	
PIZZERIA	
NEIGHBORHOOD	

TOPPINGS		
O CHEESE	O MUSHROOMS	O ONIONS
O PINEAPPLE	O BACON	O TUNA
O GREEN PEPPER	O SAUSAGE	O BLACK OLIVES
O OTHER		

CHEESE	
O GREASY	O STINGY
O SMOKEY	O STINKY
O CREAMY	O SALTY

SAUCE	
O SWEET	O SAVORY
O TANGY	O SPICY
O THIN	O CHUNKY

CHEESE TO SAUCE RATIO (CSR)

CHEESE	□□□□□□□
SAUCE	□□□□□□□

FRESHNESS

O1 O2 O3 O4 O5

CRUST SIZE	CRUST	
O THIN	O BUTTERY	O CRISPY
O MEDIUM	O SPONGY	O BUBBLY
O LARGE	O CHEWY	O OTHER

CRUST

O1 O2 O3 O4 O5

STYLE	O NY O CHICAGO O OTHER

COMMENTS

MY RATING	O1 O2 O3 O4 O5 O6 O7 O8 O9 O10	EAT AGAIN?	O YES O NO

Pizza Log

DATE	
PIZZERIA	
NEIGHBORHOOD	

TOPPINGS		
○ CHEESE	○ MUSHROOMS	○ ONIONS
○ PINEAPPLE	○ BACON	○ TUNA
○ GREEN PEPPER	○ SAUSAGE	○ BLACK OLIVES
○ OTHER		

CHEESE	
○ GREASY	○ STINGY
○ SMOKEY	○ STINKY
○ CREAMY	○ SALTY

SAUCE	
○ SWEET	○ SAVORY
○ TANGY	○ SPICY
○ THIN	○ CHUNKY

CHEESE TO SAUCE RATIO (CSR)	
CHEESE	□□□□□□□
SAUCE	□□□□□□□

FRESHNESS

○ 1 ○ 2 ○ 3 ○ 4 ○ 5

CRUST SIZE	CRUST	
○ THIN	○ BUTTERY	○ CRISPY
○ MEDIUM	○ SPONGY	○ BUBBLY
○ LARGE	○ CHEWY	○ OTHER

CRUST

○ 1 ○ 2 ○ 3 ○ 4 ○ 5

STYLE ○ NY ○ CHICAGO ○ OTHER

COMMENTS

MY RATING	○1 ○2 ○3 ○4 ○5 ○6 ○7 ○8 ○9 ○10	EAT AGAIN?	○ YES ○ NO

Pizza Log

DATE	
PIZZERIA	
NEIGHBORHOOD	

TOPPINGS

○ CHEESE	○ MUSHROOMS	○ ONIONS
○ PINEAPPLE	○ BACON	○ TUNA
○ GREEN PEPPER	○ SAUSAGE	○ BLACK OLIVES
○ OTHER		

CHEESE

○ GREASY	○ STINGY
○ SMOKEY	○ STINKY
○ CREAMY	○ SALTY

SAUCE

○ SWEET	○ SAVORY
○ TANGY	○ SPICY
○ THIN	○ CHUNKY

CHEESE TO SAUCE RATIO (CSR)

CHEESE	□□□□□□□
SAUCE	□□□□□□□

FRESHNESS

○1 ○2 ○3 ○4 ○5

CRUST SIZE

○ THIN
○ MEDIUM
○ LARGE

CRUST

○ BUTTERY	○ CRISPY
○ SPONGY	○ BUBBLY
○ CHEWY	○ OTHER

CRUST

○1 ○2 ○3 ○4 ○5

STYLE ○ NY ○ CHICAGO ○ OTHER

COMMENTS

MY RATING	○1 ○2 ○3 ○4 ○5 ○6 ○7 ○8 ○9 ○10	EAT AGAIN?	○ YES ○ NO

Pizza Log

DATE

PIZZERIA

NEIGHBORHOOD

TOPPINGS

○ CHEESE ○ MUSHROOMS ○ ONIONS

○ PINEAPPLE ○ BACON ○ TUNA

○ GREEN PEPPER ○ SAUSAGE ○ BLACK OLIVES

○ OTHER

CHEESE

○ GREASY ○ STINGY

○ SMOKEY ○ STINKY

○ CREAMY ○ SALTY

SAUCE

○ SWEET ○ SAVORY

○ TANGY ○ SPICY

○ THIN ○ CHUNKY

CHEESE TO SAUCE RATIO (CSR)

CHEESE □□□□□□□

SAUCE □□□□□□□

FRESHNESS

○1 ○2 ○3 ○4 ○5

CRUST SIZE

○ THIN

○ MEDIUM

○ LARGE

CRUST

○ BUTTERY ○ CRISPY

○ SPONGY ○ BUBBLY

○ CHEWY ○ OTHER

CRUST

○1 ○2 ○3 ○4 ○5

STYLE ○ NY ○ CHICAGO ○ OTHER

COMMENTS

MY RATING ○1 ○2 ○3 ○4 ○5 ○6 ○7 ○8 ○9 ○10

EAT AGAIN? ○ YES ○ NO

Pizza Log

DATE	
PIZZERIA	
NEIGHBORHOOD	

TOPPINGS			CHEESE	
○ CHEESE	○ MUSHROOMS	○ ONIONS	○ GREASY	○ STINGY
○ PINEAPPLE	○ BACON	○ TUNA	○ SMOKEY	○ STINKY
○ GREEN PEPPER	○ SAUSAGE	○ BLACK OLIVES	○ CREAMY	○ SALTY
○ OTHER			SAUCE	
			○ SWEET	○ SAVORY
			○ TANGY	○ SPICY
			○ THIN	○ CHUNKY
			CHEESE TO SAUCE RATIO (CSR)	
FRESHNESS			CHEESE	☐☐☐☐☐☐☐
○1 ○2 ○3 ○4 ○5			SAUCE	☐☐☐☐☐☐☐

CRUST SIZE	CRUST		CRUST	
○ THIN	○ BUTTERY	○ CRISPY	○1 ○2 ○3 ○4 ○5	
○ MEDIUM	○ SPONGY	○ BUBBLY		
○ LARGE	○ CHEWY	○ OTHER	STYLE	○ NY ○ CHICAGO ○ OTHER

COMMENTS

MY RATING	○1 ○2 ○3 ○4 ○5 ○6 ○7 ○8 ○9 ○10	EAT AGAIN?	○ YES ○ NO

Pizza Log

DATE	
PIZZERIA	
NEIGHBORHOOD	

TOPPINGS

○ CHEESE	○ MUSHROOMS	○ ONIONS
○ PINEAPPLE	○ BACON	○ TUNA
○ GREEN PEPPER	○ SAUSAGE	○ BLACK OLIVES
○ OTHER		

CHEESE

○ GREASY	○ STINGY
○ SMOKEY	○ STINKY
○ CREAMY	○ SALTY

SAUCE

○ SWEET	○ SAVORY
○ TANGY	○ SPICY
○ THIN	○ CHUNKY

CHEESE TO SAUCE RATIO (CSR)

CHEESE	□□□□□□□
SAUCE	□□□□□□□

FRESHNESS

○1 ○2 ○3 ○4 ○5

CRUST SIZE

○ THIN
○ MEDIUM
○ LARGE

CRUST

○ BUTTERY	○ CRISPY
○ SPONGY	○ BUBBLY
○ CHEWY	○ OTHER

CRUST

○1 ○2 ○3 ○4 ○5

STYLE ○ NY ○ CHICAGO ○ OTHER

COMMENTS

MY RATING ○1 ○2 ○3 ○4 ○5 ○6 ○7 ○8 ○9 ○10

EAT AGAIN? ○ YES ○ NO

Pizza Log

DATE	
PIZZERIA	
NEIGHBORHOOD	

TOPPINGS

○ CHEESE	○ MUSHROOMS	○ ONIONS
○ PINEAPPLE	○ BACON	○ TUNA
○ GREEN PEPPER	○ SAUSAGE	○ BLACK OLIVES

○ OTHER

CHEESE

○ GREASY	○ STINGY
○ SMOKEY	○ STINKY
○ CREAMY	○ SALTY

SAUCE

○ SWEET	○ SAVORY
○ TANGY	○ SPICY
○ THIN	○ CHUNKY

CHEESE TO SAUCE RATIO (CSR)

CHEESE	□ □ □ □ □ □ □
SAUCE	□ □ □ □ □ □ □

FRESHNESS

○1 ○2 ○3 ○4 ○5

CRUST SIZE

○ THIN
○ MEDIUM
○ LARGE

CRUST

○ BUTTERY	○ CRISPY
○ SPONGY	○ BUBBLY
○ CHEWY	○ OTHER

CRUST

○1 ○2 ○3 ○4 ○5

STYLE ○ NY ○ CHICAGO ○ OTHER

COMMENTS

MY RATING ○1 ○2 ○3 ○4 ○5 ○6 ○7 ○8 ○9 ○10

EAT AGAIN? ○ YES ○ NO

Pizza Log

DATE	
PIZZERIA	
NEIGHBORHOOD	

TOPPINGS		
○ CHEESE	○ MUSHROOMS	○ ONIONS
○ PINEAPPLE	○ BACON	○ TUNA
○ GREEN PEPPER	○ SAUSAGE	○ BLACK OLIVES
○ OTHER		

CHEESE	
○ GREASY	○ STINGY
○ SMOKEY	○ STINKY
○ CREAMY	○ SALTY

SAUCE	
○ SWEET	○ SAVORY
○ TANGY	○ SPICY
○ THIN	○ CHUNKY

CHEESE TO SAUCE RATIO (CSR)	
CHEESE	☐ ☐ ☐ ☐ ☐ ☐ ☐
SAUCE	☐ ☐ ☐ ☐ ☐ ☐ ☐

FRESHNESS

○1 ○2 ○3 ○4 ○5

CRUST SIZE	CRUST	
○ THIN	○ BUTTERY	○ CRISPY
○ MEDIUM	○ SPONGY	○ BUBBLY
○ LARGE	○ CHEWY	○ OTHER

CRUST

○1 ○2 ○3 ○4 ○5

STYLE	○ NY ○ CHICAGO ○ OTHER

COMMENTS

MY RATING	○1 ○2 ○3 ○4 ○5 ○6 ○7 ○8 ○9 ○10	EAT AGAIN?	○ YES ○ NO

Pizza Log

DATE	
PIZZERIA	
NEIGHBORHOOD	

TOPPINGS

○ CHEESE	○ MUSHROOMS	○ ONIONS
○ PINEAPPLE	○ BACON	○ TUNA
○ GREEN PEPPER	○ SAUSAGE	○ BLACK OLIVES
○ OTHER		

CHEESE

○ GREASY	○ STINGY
○ SMOKEY	○ STINKY
○ CREAMY	○ SALTY

SAUCE

○ SWEET	○ SAVORY
○ TANGY	○ SPICY
○ THIN	○ CHUNKY

CHEESE TO SAUCE RATIO (CSR)

CHEESE	□□□□□□□
SAUCE	□□□□□□□

FRESHNESS

○1 ○2 ○3 ○4 ○5

CRUST SIZE

○ THIN
○ MEDIUM
○ LARGE

CRUST

○ BUTTERY	○ CRISPY
○ SPONGY	○ BUBBLY
○ CHEWY	○ OTHER

CRUST

○1 ○2 ○3 ○4 ○5

STYLE ○ NY ○ CHICAGO ○ OTHER

COMMENTS

MY RATING ○1 ○2 ○3 ○4 ○5 ○6 ○7 ○8 ○9 ○10

EAT AGAIN? ○ YES ○ NO

Pizza Log

DATE	
PIZZERIA	
NEIGHBORHOOD	

TOPPINGS		
○ CHEESE	○ MUSHROOMS	○ ONIONS
○ PINEAPPLE	○ BACON	○ TUNA
○ GREEN PEPPER	○ SAUSAGE	○ BLACK OLIVES
○ OTHER		

CHEESE	
○ GREASY	○ STINGY
○ SMOKEY	○ STINKY
○ CREAMY	○ SALTY

SAUCE	
○ SWEET	○ SAVORY
○ TANGY	○ SPICY
○ THIN	○ CHUNKY

CHEESE TO SAUCE RATIO (CSR)	
CHEESE	☐☐☐☐☐☐☐
SAUCE	☐☐☐☐☐☐☐

FRESHNESS

○ 1 ○ 2 ○ 3 ○ 4 ○ 5

CRUST SIZE	CRUST	
○ THIN	○ BUTTERY	○ CRISPY
○ MEDIUM	○ SPONGY	○ BUBBLY
○ LARGE	○ CHEWY	○ OTHER

CRUST

○ 1 ○ 2 ○ 3 ○ 4 ○ 5

STYLE	○ NY ○ CHICAGO ○ OTHER

COMMENTS

MY RATING	○1 ○2 ○3 ○4 ○5 ○6 ○7 ○8 ○9 ○10	EAT AGAIN?	○ YES ○ NO

Pizza Log

DATE	
PIZZERIA	
NEIGHBORHOOD	

TOPPINGS

○ CHEESE	○ MUSHROOMS	○ ONIONS
○ PINEAPPLE	○ BACON	○ TUNA
○ GREEN PEPPER	○ SAUSAGE	○ BLACK OLIVES
○ OTHER		

CHEESE

○ GREASY	○ STINGY
○ SMOKEY	○ STINKY
○ CREAMY	○ SALTY

SAUCE

○ SWEET	○ SAVORY
○ TANGY	○ SPICY
○ THIN	○ CHUNKY

CHEESE TO SAUCE RATIO (CSR)

CHEESE	☐☐☐☐☐☐☐
SAUCE	☐☐☐☐☐☐☐

FRESHNESS

○1 ○2 ○3 ○4 ○5

CRUST SIZE

○ THIN
○ MEDIUM
○ LARGE

CRUST

○ BUTTERY	○ CRISPY
○ SPONGY	○ BUBBLY
○ CHEWY	○ OTHER

CRUST

○1 ○2 ○3 ○4 ○5

STYLE ○ NY ○ CHICAGO ○ OTHER

COMMENTS

MY RATING	○1 ○2 ○3 ○4 ○5 ○6 ○7 ○8 ○9 ○10	EAT AGAIN?	○ YES ○ NO

Pizza Log

DATE	
PIZZERIA	
NEIGHBORHOOD	

TOPPINGS

○ CHEESE	○ MUSHROOMS	○ ONIONS
○ PINEAPPLE	○ BACON	○ TUNA
○ GREEN PEPPER	○ SAUSAGE	○ BLACK OLIVES
○ OTHER		

CHEESE

○ GREASY	○ STINGY
○ SMOKEY	○ STINKY
○ CREAMY	○ SALTY

SAUCE

○ SWEET	○ SAVORY
○ TANGY	○ SPICY
○ THIN	○ CHUNKY

CHEESE TO SAUCE RATIO (CSR)

CHEESE	□□□□□□□
SAUCE	□□□□□□□

FRESHNESS

○1 ○2 ○3 ○4 ○5

CRUST SIZE

○ THIN
○ MEDIUM
○ LARGE

CRUST

○ BUTTERY	○ CRISPY
○ SPONGY	○ BUBBLY
○ CHEWY	○ OTHER

CRUST

○1 ○2 ○3 ○4 ○5

STYLE ○ NY ○ CHICAGO ○ OTHER

COMMENTS

MY RATING	○1 ○2 ○3 ○4 ○5 ○6 ○7 ○8 ○9 ○10	EAT AGAIN?	○ YES ○ NO

Pizza Log

DATE	
PIZZERIA	
NEIGHBORHOOD	

TOPPINGS

O CHEESE	O MUSHROOMS	O ONIONS
O PINEAPPLE	O BACON	O TUNA
O GREEN PEPPER	O SAUSAGE	O BLACK OLIVES
O OTHER		

CHEESE

O GREASY	O STINGY
O SMOKEY	O STINKY
O CREAMY	O SALTY

SAUCE

O SWEET	O SAVORY
O TANGY	O SPICY
O THIN	O CHUNKY

CHEESE TO SAUCE RATIO (CSR)

CHEESE	☐☐☐☐☐☐☐
SAUCE	☐☐☐☐☐☐☐

FRESHNESS

O1 O2 O3 O4 O5

CRUST SIZE

O THIN
O MEDIUM
O LARGE

CRUST

O BUTTERY	O CRISPY
O SPONGY	O BUBBLY
O CHEWY	O OTHER

CRUST

O1 O2 O3 O4 O5

STYLE	O NY O CHICAGO O OTHER

COMMENTS

MY RATING	O1 O2 O3 O4 O5 O6 O7 O8 O9 O10	EAT AGAIN?	O YES O NO

Pizza Log

DATE	
PIZZERIA	
NEIGHBORHOOD	

TOPPINGS

○ CHEESE	○ MUSHROOMS	○ ONIONS
○ PINEAPPLE	○ BACON	○ TUNA
○ GREEN PEPPER	○ SAUSAGE	○ BLACK OLIVES
○ OTHER		

CHEESE

○ GREASY	○ STINGY
○ SMOKEY	○ STINKY
○ CREAMY	○ SALTY

SAUCE

○ SWEET	○ SAVORY
○ TANGY	○ SPICY
○ THIN	○ CHUNKY

CHEESE TO SAUCE RATIO (CSR)

CHEESE	☐☐☐☐☐☐☐
SAUCE	☐☐☐☐☐☐☐

FRESHNESS

○1 ○2 ○3 ○4 ○5

CRUST SIZE

○ THIN
○ MEDIUM
○ LARGE

CRUST

○ BUTTERY	○ CRISPY
○ SPONGY	○ BUBBLY
○ CHEWY	○ OTHER

CRUST

○1 ○2 ○3 ○4 ○5

STYLE ○ NY ○ CHICAGO ○ OTHER

COMMENTS

MY RATING ○1 ○2 ○3 ○4 ○5 ○6 ○7 ○8 ○9 ○10

EAT AGAIN? ○ YES ○ NO

Pizza Log

DATE	
PIZZERIA	
NEIGHBORHOOD	

TOPPINGS

○ CHEESE	○ MUSHROOMS	○ ONIONS
○ PINEAPPLE	○ BACON	○ TUNA
○ GREEN PEPPER	○ SAUSAGE	○ BLACK OLIVES
○ OTHER		

CHEESE

○ GREASY	○ STINGY
○ SMOKEY	○ STINKY
○ CREAMY	○ SALTY

SAUCE

○ SWEET	○ SAVORY
○ TANGY	○ SPICY
○ THIN	○ CHUNKY

CHEESE TO SAUCE RATIO (CSR)

CHEESE	☐ ☐ ☐ ☐ ☐ ☐ ☐
SAUCE	☐ ☐ ☐ ☐ ☐ ☐ ☐

FRESHNESS

○ 1 ○ 2 ○ 3 ○ 4 ○ 5

CRUST SIZE

○ THIN
○ MEDIUM
○ LARGE

CRUST

○ BUTTERY	○ CRISPY
○ SPONGY	○ BUBBLY
○ CHEWY	○ OTHER

CRUST

○ 1 ○ 2 ○ 3 ○ 4 ○ 5

STYLE ○ NY ○ CHICAGO ○ OTHER

COMMENTS

MY RATING ○ 1 ○ 2 ○ 3 ○ 4 ○ 5 ○ 6 ○ 7 ○ 8 ○ 9 ○ 10

EAT AGAIN? ○ YES ○ NO

Lightning Source UK Ltd.
Milton Keynes UK
UKHW030635170720
366698UK00010B/1540

9 781649 301864